Fun Family Traditions

Cynthia MacGregor

Meadowbrook Press

Distributed by Simon & Schuster
New York

Library of Congress Cataloging-in-Publication Data
MacGregor, Cynthia.
    Fun family traditions: over 100 fun activities to bring your family
    closer together/[Cynthia MacGregor].
        p.   cm.
    ISBN 0-88166-363-8 (Meadowbrook)—0-671-31816-0 (Simon &
    Schuster)
        1. Family—Miscellanea. 2. Family recreation. 3. Creative activities
    and seat work. 4. Holidays. I. Title
    HQ734 .M152 2000
    306.85—dc21   99-057877
                                                                   CIP

Managing Editor: Christine Zuchora-Walske
Copyeditors: Joseph Gredler, Jason Sanford
Production Manager: Joe Gagne
Desktop Publishing: Danielle White
Illustrations: Jack Lindstrom

Published by Meadowbrook Press, 5451 Smetana Drive, Minnetonka,
Minnesota 55343

www.meadowbrookpress.com

BOOK TRADE DISTRIBUTION by Simon & Schuster, a division of
Simon and Schuster, Inc., 1230 Avenue of the Americas, New York,
NY 10020

04 03 02 01 00   10 9 8 7 6 5 4 3 2 1

Printed in the United States of America

Dedication

for Justin and Tori, as always,
and now Steffan, too.
May you always have lots of family fun!

Acknowledgments

Thanks, as always, to good friend and colleague Vic Bobb.

Contents

Preserving Family History: Family Knowledge Activities

Crafting Family Traditions

Family Pastimes

Fun Family Holidays

Introduction

Maybe it's been one of those days: Your teenage daughter thinks you're hopelessly old-fashioned because you still say "groovy" and you won't let her attend a coed sleepover. Your seven-year-old son came home from school saying, "Why can't we be like Lee's family? They do such cool stuff!" And your eleven-year old sounds like a broken record. All she can say is "Buy me a Barbie. . . . Buy me a new sweater. . . . Buy me a pony. . . . Buy me a new CD."

You try to enforce the rules you believe to be fair and reasonable. You try not to embarrass your kids in front of their friends. You've certainly bent over backward to buy them things they've wanted over the years, even when your budget—and your desire to not spoil your kids—said no. You've probably stood in a long line on a windy, wintry sidewalk on the rawest December day hoping to be one of the lucky few to walk away with a limited-edition toy. And Santa probably got all the credit for your effort.

You love your kids and you want them to feel that they are an important part of your family's traditions and experiences. You want them to want to do things with each other, to laugh at inside jokes, and to feel proud to belong to their family. In short, you want your hard work and undying devotion to result in a happy, tight-knit group.

I believe this book will help you strengthen the bonds that might feel strained right now. The activities and rituals on the following pages will help bring you closer together. You and your kids will learn interesting things about your family's history and will do fun things together. And this will help reaffirm a solid sense of belonging to a cohesive family unit. There are few things more precious.

Have fun!

Cynthia

Preserving Family History: Family Knowledge Activities

Family Tree

Today, families are often spread across a country or the world, and many people know their relatives only as faceless names. Most people are familiar with just their immediate relatives—parents, grandparents, aunts, uncles, and first cousins. Distant relatives have become even more distant, and many have been forgotten entirely. Few people know the names of their great-grandparents. What a pity!

A family tree will help you rediscover your roots. You'll also learn a lot about your trunk, branches, and stray leaves. A family tree is a fun way to establish a sense of historical connectedness as you travel back in time and across vast distances.

Materials:
- Paper
- Pen, pencil, or fine-line marker
- Glue or paste, photographs, and scissors (optional)

Directions:
1. Put a piece of paper sideways on the desk or table in front of you. At the top of the paper, about a third of the way in from the left, write one parent's mother's full maiden name ("Nancy Jane O'Reilly") and father's full name ("Morton David Bell"). Write the names next to each other and connect them with a short horizontal line. *Note:* If any women in your family kept their maiden names after marriage, or any men changed theirs, you might want to indicate that following the names.

2. Draw a short vertical line down from the connecting line.

3. If parent one is an only child, write his name where the vertical line ends. If he has any brothers or sisters, draw a horizontal line there.

4. For parent one and each of his sisters or brothers, draw a short vertical line down from that horizontal line. Write a sister's or a brother's name where each vertical line ends. Put parent one's name the farthest to the right. Leave plenty of space between the names.

5. Draw a short horizontal line, like a hyphen, next to each sister's or brother's name. Write the full birth-given name of the spouse of each sister or brother on the other side of each hyphen. (If the sister or brother has no spouse, leave the space blank.)

6. If the sister or brother is widowed or divorced, write the name of the divorced or dead spouse in parentheses. If the sister or brother has remarried, write the new spouse's name on the other side of the sister or brother, again with a short horizontal line connecting the two names.

7. Display the children of this generation the same way you showed the children of parent one's generation.

8. Do the same thing for the other parent's family on the right side of the paper. Make parent two's name the one farthest to the left, near parent one's name.

9. Draw a horizontal line connecting the two parents, and a vertical line below which you'll show all the kids in your family.

10. If you like, paste a small picture of each relative next to his or her name. If you have old pictures and no negatives, that's OK. Photo labs can make copies without having the negatives, so you don't have to cut up one-of-a-kind, irreplaceable pictures.

11. You can go back as far as you like, including grandparents, great-grandparents, great-great-grandparents, and all their siblings and children. But the farther back you go, the more paper you will need. You can also create your family tree on a computer using any of several easy-to-use family-history programs available at most computer stores.

Helpful Hint: Since this project lends itself to older children and adults, help younger kids feel included by having them draw pictures of relatives and extended family.

Timeline

Add perspective to your family history by creating a family timeline. You'll have fun discovering what happened when to whom. There are three kinds of timelines you can make. In each case, you'll draw a long, straight line marked with dates at appropriate intervals. Beside these dates you'll write significant family events.

The first timeline is specific to your immediate family. It could, for example, start with the year Mom and Dad got married and could include a year for each child's birth and other significant milestones. You could confine the timeline to major milestones such as religious ceremonies (first communion, baptism, or bar mitzvah), the year when each child started school, and family moves. You could also include minor events such as the date Kayla learned to ride a bicycle without training wheels, the date Jon joined the Cub Scouts, Beth's first summer camp, and so on.

The second type of timeline includes your whole extended family (aunts, uncles, cousins, and so on). This timeline usually shows only births, deaths, marriages, and divorces within the larger family. However, you could also include other significant events if you like.

The third type of timeline relates the significant events in your family to significant world events. For example, 1963 could be shown as both the year President Kennedy was shot and the year Grandma Ruth and Grandpa Lou got married.

Materials:
- Several sheets of paper
- Pen, pencil, or fine-line marker
- Adhesive tape

Directions:
1. Tape four or more sheets of paper together end to end. Graph paper is useful for this project.
2. Draw a straight line across the papers.
3. Decide on a starting date for the timeline. Make a small vertical mark at the extreme left of the horizontal line and write the year and the event that took place that year. Write event information in narrow columns under the date.

4. Repeat the directions above for subsequent events. Separate the events with appropriate spacing.

5. As time goes on, you can add more paper to the right side. That way you can extend your timeline and record important events as they occur.

6. Tape your timeline to a long wall (perhaps in a hallway). Make sure it is low enough that everyone can read it easily. You can also fold the timeline up and keep it in a special album or family-history book.

7. If you make the world-events timeline, use different-colored pens to differentiate between family events and other important events.

Helpful Hint: This project also lends itself to older children and adults, so look for ways to include the younger kids.

Family Journal

One way to preserve treasured family memories is by writing them down in a journal. You should establish a regular pattern that works for everybody—nightly, weekly, or monthly. Unlike a diary, which is private and often deals with sensitive personal issues, a journal is for the entire family and is more likely to deal with events. But that doesn't mean you should avoid emotional issues!

Each family member can take a turn writing in the journal, or nominate the person with the neatest handwriting to record the events dictated by the family. What were the important events of the day, week, or month? Did the family do anything special together? Did any member of the family do anything special that's worth remembering? Did a family pet do anything memorable?

Even small events count. Did Ross cook a hamburger for the first time? Did Pat make a new friend? Did Spot get loose and have the family searching for him for an hour? It's all suitable material for the journal.

Materials:
- Blank book or notebook
- Pen

Directions:
1. Gather regularly, at least once a month, for the specific purpose of recording memorable events. Try not to let other agendas interfere.

2. Agree on who will record the journal entries.

3. Every family member can contribute ideas. Mom or Dad may need to be the final arbiter of what is included.

4. From time to time, gather to read journal entries from the past. You may wish to read the entries from this week last year, this week the year before, and so on at regular intervals.

Helpful Hint: You can use the journal to answer questions or settle disputes when you can't remember what year you got the two pet birds or whether it was at the Labor Day picnic or the Memorial Day picnic that the ants got into the potato salad.

Family Scrapbook

In addition to preserving memories in the Family Journal (page 6), also keep a scrapbook to save specific items that will spark family memories. Mementos will be easy to archive if they are reasonably flat and can be attached to a page. You might add a written description that explains the item's significance. Since you probably won't acquire mementos at regular intervals, put them in the scrapbook as you get them.

Materials:
- Large scrapbook
- Double-faced poster tape or glue
- Pen

Directions:
1. Save mementos such as the following:
   - Ticket stubs from the ice show, ball game, and circus
   - Postcards from various vacation destinations
   - A pressed flower from the unusual bush in Aunt Helen's yard
   - Items brought back from your trip out west
   - Anything else that's reasonably flat and will inspire family memories

2. Tape or glue each item to a page in the scrapbook. (Each item does not necessarily need its own page.)

3. Write a note about each item. This can be as brief as "Family saw Ringling Brothers Circus March 23, 2000." The entry can contain as much or as little information as you want.

4. From time to time, look back at the scrapbook and reminisce. This can be a scheduled family event or just an idle individual pleasure.

Helpful Hint: Help younger kids insert items into the scrapbook neatly, and encourage everyone to turn the pages carefully.

Time Capsule

Why not create a time capsule when a child is born into your family? There's no need to bury this time capsule or embed it in the cornerstone of the new house you're building—just stow it in some out-of-the-way location for viewing at a later date.

Materials:
- One large box for each child
- Suggested contents described below

Directions:
1. Gather some or all of the following items (plus whatever else seems appropriate) and place them in a large box:
   - Birth notices that appeared in the local newspaper, Mom's or Dad's company newsletter, or any other information source
   - A copy of the birth announcement you mailed out
   - A deflated IT'S A GIRL/BOY balloon
   - An IT'S A GIRL/BOY band from a celebratory cigar
   - Congratulatory cards and e-mail you received
   - The wristband the baby wore in the hospital
   - One of the socks that fit on the baby's feet when she was a newborn (or some other article of clothing)
   - A picture of the baby
   - A photo of the baby's room as it looked the day he first came home from the hospital; a photo of the outside of the house as it looked that day; and perhaps one of your street and several of the inside of the house including the living room, kitchen, your bedroom, and other rooms
   - Photos of the entire family including your pet(s)
   - A paragraph-long list of your aspirations for the baby—your hopes and dreams of what you want her to get out of life, to be in life, and to have in life
   - A description of any religious ceremony you may have had for the baby accompanied by an audiotaped or videotaped recording
   - A tape recording of every family member welcoming the new arrival and expressing thoughts and feelings on the birth
   - A list of the baby gifts, including the names of the givers

- A copy of the hospital and doctor's bills (You'll laugh at the low amounts in years to come.)
- A newspaper from the child's date of birth showing the major events of the day—globally, nationally, and locally
- A national magazine from that week, showing what was going on in the world at the time as well as what products were being advertised (The pictures—both those accompanying news stories and those in ads—will be of interest later, showing what people were wearing, driving, and playing with, and what it all cost at the time.)
- Movie reviews, book reviews, theater reviews, concert reviews, or even software reviews, for a better feel of what was happening at the time and what was popular
- The sports section of the paper for that date as well as sports trading cards issued that year, showing who the major players were in the different major-league sports
- A toy catalogue showing what toys were popular at the time
- A tape of the baby gurgling, cooing, and crying
- The baby's footprint and handprint

2. Put the box away and avoid the temptation to open it and peek in too early.

3. Open it at a suitable milestone such as the eighteenth or twenty-first birthday, high school or college graduation, wedding day, or first day on the job.

Helpful Hint: Even if you've already had your kids and don't plan on any more, it may not be too late to assemble at least some of the suggested items for a belated time capsule.

Family Newspaper

A family newspaper is a great way to get the news out about goings-on in your family. When determining how often you might "publish," you should consider the size of your extended family, how close the kids are to their cousins and other relatives, and how much takes place that's worth reporting. You could send your newspaper out weekly, monthly, quarterly, annually, or as the occasion demands.

For this project, you and your kids will need to get in touch with counterparts in other branches of the family. Have the kids interview their cousins to learn any new or fun information about family happenings. Once you have a good chunk of news, publish the newspaper and send a copy to everyone in your extended family.

Materials:
- Telephone or computer (for e-mail) for getting in touch with various branches of the family
- Typewriter (or computer) and paper for creating the newspaper
- Envelopes and stamps for mailing out copies of the newspaper to other branches of the family (unless you're using e-mail)
- Pen and paper for taking notes during phone interviews
- Copy machine (or access to one) if you don't have a computer and printer

Directions:
1. Call or e-mail all the other branches of your extended family and get their latest news. Is there a new car, new pet, or new baby? Did anyone graduate from school or get a new job or promotion? Did anyone join Scouts, take part in a ballet recital, start piano lessons, or get visited by an old friend who had previously moved out of town? Has anyone visited Disney World, gone to see relatives, or taken a class trip to Washington D.C.? Get the details.

2. Write each piece of news as a separate article. Or, if you have only a sentence or two to write about many of the news items, write one article covering all the news in each branch of the family. Remember that each article needs a title such as "Dayton Family Gets New Cat" or "Iowa Powell Family News."

3. It's not necessary to get fancy. If you're proficient with your computer and want to do two or even three columns with inserted pictures, fancy effects, and so on, you certainly can. But you can also print straightforward blocks of type that run across the page without fancy doodads. If you have a printer, you can print all the copies you need, or you can use a copy machine. Those using a typewriter can make copies for each branch of the family. Remember, getting the news out is the main goal. Your family newspaper doesn't need to look like *The New York Times*.

4. Hand-deliver or mail a copy of the newspaper to each branch of the family.

5. If you have neither a computer nor easy access to a copy machine, simply type one copy of the newspaper with instructions for each branch of the family to forward it to the next after reading it. (Supply a list of names and addresses.)

6. If your family is already hooked up to the Internet, consider sending out an e-mail version of the newspaper. Not only is this faster than a traditional newspaper, it saves paper and money.

Helpful Hint: It's fun to get the kids involved by having them do phone interviews, but make sure to confirm all information before publishing.

Write the Family History

There's more to your family's history than dates. Knowing when and where each family member was born is a good start, but why stop there? You should include lots of human-interest stories, too.

Materials:
- Paper and pen
- Tape recorder, typewriter or computer, ring binder or construction paper, and staples or binder clip (all optional)

Directions:
1. Talk to as many adult family members as you can. Include parents, grandparents, great-grandparents if they're still alive, aunts and uncles, and adult cousins. Ask questions about the family, including past generations, and carefully write down the answers or tape-record them. You could ask questions such as the following: Who was the first person in the family to go to college? Are there any especially colorful family members? Are there any famous ones? Are there any locally prominent people—maybe a town mayor or a popular school principal?

2. Organize the answers into some logical form (chronologically, for example). You may want to construct chapters for stories such as the following: events on Mom's side of the family before she was born, events on Dad's side before he was born, Mom's childhood, Dad's childhood, events in the immediate family after Mom and Dad got married, or events in the extended family that occurred during those married years.

3. You can write the finished book in longhand or type it on a computer or typewriter. You could attach the pages between construction paper covers with a binder clip or staples or put them in a ring binder. If you really want the book to look nice, have it professionally printed and bound.

4. Keep adding to the family history whenever you talk to family members with whom you haven't had contact recently.

Helpful Hint: Even the family members you're not especially proud of should have a place in your family history.

Illustrated Family History

Pictures make words come alive, and kids love picture books. Why not write family stories illustrated with pictures drawn by the kids? Maybe there's a funny story about Gramma Edna having to chase the cow out of her petunias. Or maybe Uncle Joey went fishing one day, as a child, when he was supposed to be in school . . . and he ran into his dad at the lake! Collect these stories from family members, write them down, and draw pictures of the stories to go with the words.

Never mind if no one can draw Grandma Edna accurately, or if the lake doesn't look at all as Uncle Joey remembers it. The important thing is that everyone will remember the stories better when there are pictures to go with them.

Materials:
- Paper and pen (or typewriter or computer)
- Crayons or colored fine-line markers
- Ring binder or construction paper, and staples or binder clip

Directions:
1. Ask everyone in your extended family for funny, amazing, heart-warming, or otherwise interesting stories about family members.
2. Write them down or type them up.
3. Draw at least one picture to illustrate each story.
4. Make the book by creating a front and back cover out of construction paper and stapling or clipping the pages together, or by putting them in a ring binder.

Helpful Hint: If your kids don't particularly like drawing and painting, they might enjoy making a picture book using family photos. Create the book as explained above, then substitute photographs for the illustrations.

Family Recipe Book: Heirloom Recipes

While you're compiling your family history, don't forget the recipes. After all, most family get-togethers involve eating.

Members of the extended family are probably well known for certain recipes. If Grandma's banana bread, Aunt Julia's hot dog casserole, or Uncle Frank's firehouse chili are family favorites, collect the recipes and include them in this book.

Materials:
- Loose-leaf paper
- Loose-leaf notebook
- Pen

Directions:
1. Call or write to each member of the extended family. Ask for one or more recipes that the family likes or that a particular family member is proud of.
2. Get precise instructions for preparing each recipe.
3. Write down each recipe on a separate sheet of loose-leaf paper and integrate the pages into one book.
4. If you've collected enough recipes to divide the cookbook into sections, do so. You'll probably want to separate meat, vegetables, potatoes, desserts, soups, and so on. However, you might want to organize the recipes according to where they came from, so that each relative would get his or her own section.
5. Give your cookbook a name that's unique to your family. Note all the editors and contributors, and draw a decorative picture or design on the cover.

Helpful Hint: You can make color copies of the cookbook for all members of the extended family by using a color printer or having a professional printer do the job.

Family Recipe Book for Kids

Do your kids enjoy cooking and helping in the kitchen? Are they sometimes frustrated that many foods are beyond their abilities to prepare, even with parental help? Have them compile a family recipe book of kid-friendly recipes.

Materials:
- Loose-leaf paper
- Loose-leaf notebook
- Pen
- Colored marking pens

Directions:

1. Write down the instructions for preparing each meal that your kids will enjoy making and eating. Put each recipe on a separate page. These can be as simple as open-faced sandwiches with carrot facial features, or as complex as baking an entire cake from scratch. The kids may already know some of the recipes by heart, and they can get others from you or from cookbooks in your kitchen.

2. Have your kids talk to their cousins and relatives to get additional kid-friendly recipes. How about celery sticks stuffed with peanut butter and raisins? Or sugar cookies? Or hot dogs wrapped in bacon? Write down each recipe on a separate page, being sure to include precise ingredients and cooking instructions.

3. As you accumulate more and more recipes, you may want to divide the book into sections such as sandwiches, desserts, hot lunches, dinner meats, or any other categories your kids like. You might want to separate simpler recipes from more complex ones, or recipes that require cooking from those that don't.

4. Using one or more colored marking pens, title your cookbook and write the editors' and contributors' names on the cover. Decorate with pictures or fun photos of kids in the kitchen.

Helpful Hint: Parents should carefully supervise all meal preparations, especially those involving knives and appliances.

Book of Family Games

Does your family sometimes forget some of the best games they've played? You might want to assemble a book that details your favorite games. Rather than buying a game book you might or might not like, written by someone who doesn't know your family, you can write your own book! Accent the book with funny stories about the games themselves and what happened to family members while playing.

Materials:
- Paper, pen, fine-line markers
- Two sheets of pale-colored construction paper, stapler

Directions:
1. Gather the family together to write down a list of all the games the family enjoys playing. You might want to include board or boxed games, but focus on ones that aren't prepackaged. The best games might be the ones the family invented. Have one or more secretaries take notes on titles and rules.

2. Ask the family if anyone remembers any funny stories associated with any of the games. Wasn't Sardines the game the family played when the cousins from Duluth came to visit? Remember how cousin John sneezed when everyone was hiding behind the shed? Write down all the stories, or use a tape recorder and write them down later.

3. Have the family continue thinking of games and memories, and ask extended family members to write or call with more information.

4. When you're satisfied with the number of games and memories, it's time to compile the book. Place one game on each page. Include titles and rules first, then add any stories you might have. Staple or clip the pages together. You might want to divide the book into chapters, depending on the size of your book.

5. Create a fancy cover with construction paper and markers.

6. Make copies of the book for other branches of the family using a copy machine or computer printer.

Helpful Hint: Access to a computer makes compiling and organizing the book much easier.

Book of Family Travel Games

How does your family amuse itself on car trips? Do you play Geography, count license plates from other states, form sentences out of the letters on passing license plates, count to one hundred by threes, or play I Spy? Show the world how creative you are! Write your family's very own travel game book! Any family of wiggleworm kids and hair-pulling parents (and isn't that all of us when it's time to take a car trip?) would be grateful to have your suggestions.

Materials:
- Paper
- Pen (or computer or typewriter)
- Construction paper
- Fine-line markers
- Stapler

Directions:
1. Gather the family together to generate a list of all the games the family enjoys playing in the car. Have one or more members take notes on the titles and rules.

2. Ask family members to continue thinking of car games, and have them write or call you with more information.

3. Write or type detailed instructions from the notes. You'll probably want to separate games one per page. Staple pages together.

4. Create fancy cover pages using construction paper and markers.

5. Make copies of the book for all who want them. If you've hand-written or typed it, photocopy the pages. If you've used a computer, simply print out additional copies.

6. In addition to giving copies to family members, you can sell them at a lemonade stand in front of your house, or sell them during the next yard sale.

Helpful Hint: Don't forget to take the book on vacation with you!

Passing on Heirlooms

Many families attach enormous value to family artifacts, even when they're not worth much money. There's no monetary value to the ticket stubs from the Frank Sinatra concert where your father proposed to your mother, but they're very important to your family. Great-Grandma's diamond brooch carries the added value of being worth a lot of money, but that's not the only reason you treasure it.

Why not perform a ceremony to hand down precious heirlooms to your kids? Choosing who gets what can be tricky, and I don't pretend to have an easy way around that. But once you've made these difficult decisions, transferring family treasures can be a wonderful family event.

Materials:
• Family treasures that you wish to hand down to your kids

Directions:
1. Decide how big a deal you want the ceremony to be. I've provided some suggestions that you can modify however you see fit.

2. Make a special dinner to precede the ceremony. Choose a favorite old recipe to add meaning to the event.

3. After dinner, get out the family photo albums and find pictures of an event connected with the item you're handing down, or pictures of Great-Grandma wearing the brooch—whatever is available.

4. Get out the family scrapbook, too, so you can look at other mementos related to the heirloom.

5. Retell family stories that explain the special value of the heirloom.

6. If a particular item was handed down to you, recount the circumstances under which it came into your possession. Did Grandma say anything special when she entrusted you with Granddad's Bible? Did Aunt Edith explain why you were the one being given Uncle Harry's fishing pole?

7. Say a few words about preserving the family's legacy.

8. Take a picture of your child holding the treasured item. You can also preserve the ceremony on videotape or audiotape.

Helpful Hint: Invite all the family members to this special ceremony, and try to have something for everybody.

Family Memory Night

Whether it's a regular or spontaneous occasion in your household, reminiscing about the special memories your family shares is wonderful. The experiences you revisit will remind each family member how special it is to belong to your family. The kids can take a break from arguing about whose turn it is to take out the garbage and whether Jennifer really did something gross to Jason's fork. Instead, they can sit back and bask in the warmth of family memories.

Materials:
- A special family location
- Popcorn or some other snack (optional)
- A fire in the fireplace (optional)

Directions:
1. Set aside a block of time for the family to gather. It can be a regular time like every Sunday night after Family Council Meeting (page 65), or the first Saturday afternoon of every month. This can also be an impromptu activity.

2. Gather someplace comfortable so nobody fidgets because his chair is too hard.

3. If you like, pop some popcorn or prepare other snacks or treats. Light a fire in the fireplace and make sure to turn off the TV.

4. Start reminiscing. You can ask each child to share a favorite family memory, or you can ask each child to share a memory of a particular topic. These might include family vacations, the day you moved into the new house, the big family reunion two years ago, or the first day of school. You can be less structured and let everyone jump in when something special occurs to them, instead of picking a topic or calling on each child by turn. Make sure everyone gets a chance to tell a story.

Helpful Hint: If one or more of your kids is shy, you can usually elicit a contribution by asking specific questions.

Childhood Memory Night

Gather near the fireplace or out on the porch in summer, break out the popcorn, and turn off the TV so it doesn't compete with your voices. It's Childhood Memory Night, a time for all to remember the good times they had when they were kids.

Materials:
• Paper and pen, tape recorder (optional)

Directions:
1. Ask everyone, especially the kids, to contribute favorite childhood memories. Family members should take turns telling stories so everyone hears and is heard.

2. Ideally, these memories should involve the whole family or at least more than just the person who's talking.

3. If you want, tape-record the stories and type or write them up later. Memories can fade quickly, so it's important to write down the precious stories shared during Childhood Memory Night so they can be passed down into the next generation's Family History (page 12) or Illustrated Family History (page 13).

Helpful Hint: Choose a room or outdoor setting that lends itself to storytelling. It's important that everyone hear as easily as possible so no one gets bored or restless.

Stories from the Past

One night a week, instead of reading from a favorite book or telling a favorite fairy tale, tell family stories. These can be from generations ago or stories about the kids when they were young. Make sure to include stories about the kids during their infant and toddler years.

Materials:
- Memories of family experiences

Directions:

1. After the kids are tucked in or gathered in the storytelling room, tell them one or more interesting family stories. These could include funny tales like the one about Great-Grandma Sara and the chicken. They could also involve more serious experiences such as how Great-Grandpa Paul changed his name after arriving in America because he was making a new life free from the persecution of his homeland.

2. Vary the stories from week to week. Occasionally include stories from your own childhood and generations ago. And don't forget to include stories from your kids' early childhood.

Helpful Hint: Do some research to discover facts about your family that will be cherished by your children.

Visit to the Past

Did Mom, Dad, Grandma, or Grandpa grow up near where you currently live? Do you have relatives "back home" and occasionally go there with the kids on vacation? If so, here's another activity that can help bring family stories to life.

It's fun for kids to imagine their parents as young kids going to school, getting into fights, moaning about teachers, having misunderstandings with their parents, and so on. It will be even more enjoyable for kids to learn about their parents' childhoods by seeing the places where their parents grew up.

Materials:
- Car or public transportation (or plane or train, if necessary)
- The places where parents grew up

Directions:
1. Pile the family in the car and go for a drive to the place where you grew up.
2. Point out the scenes from your childhood with both historical facts and personal stories. Tell them things like "Here's where the candy store used to be. I remember when I stole a candy bar. Dad—your grandpa, that is—made me go back and own up to Mr. Jacobson that I'd stolen it. He made me work to pay for it." Or you could say "Here's where I threw the snowball at Chris, but I missed and hit the minister by accident." Or "Here's where Mrs. Murphy's dog got hit by a car. I picked up the dog and ran five blocks to the vet. The vet said I probably saved the dog's life." Hearing these stories and seeing where they happened will give your kids strong memories of your past and will help them feel more closely linked to your life.

Helpful Hint: Make sure you get as close as possible to scenes from your childhood. Don't be afraid to get out of the car and walk around.

Highway to the Past

This game is similar to the preceding activity, but will work even if the kids can't be taken physically to the places where their parents grew up. Also, the kids play a more active role in this activity. They get to challenge their parents—and isn't that always fun?—in a game that will help pass the time on a long car trip.

Materials:
• Car

Directions:

1. If possible, drive on secondary roads rather than interstates or major highways. It's best if you can see more than trees or billboards.

2. First, have the kids point to anything they see along the way: a firehouse, large dog, barn, factory, and so on. Have them name what they see.

3. Next, one of the parents must provide a childhood memory somehow connected to such an item. (It doesn't have to be about that particular barn or firehouse, of course, just one like it.) If one parent can't tell a story, then the other parent can give it a try.

4. If both parents fail to supply a childhood memory, the kids win the round. Of course, the kids also win if a parent tells a story, because they get to learn more about that parent's past.

Helpful Hint: Occasionally, if you're running out of true stories and your kids approve, you might tell made-up stories or relate experiences that happened to your childhood friends.

Family Interviews

This activity is similar to Write the Family History (page 12), which concentrates primarily on facts such as when Great-Grandpa Lou came to America or where Mom and Dad's wedding was held. However, a compelling family history must also present the people behind the facts. To do this, have your kids interview their elders. These talks will produce stories that reach far beyond the simple facts the family already knows.

Materials:
- Pen and paper
- Tape recorder, typewriter, or computer (optional)

Directions:
1. Have your kids ask various relatives questions such as the following:
   - What were your favorite childhood toys?
   - How did your family celebrate holidays when you were a kid?
   - How did you celebrate birthdays?
   - What was your most memorable birthday party?
   - What was your favorite game?
   - What did you do in the evenings before there was TV?
   - How else was your childhood different from a typical childhood now?
   - Did you go trick-or-treating for Halloween? Do you remember what you dressed up as?
   - What chores were you required to do?
   - How did your schools differ from school these days?
   - How did you spend your summers?

2. Compile the answers in a book or include them as part of a family-history book.

Helpful Hint: Make sure you confirm that the information your kids acquire is accurately reported to you. Double-check with family members if necessary.

Nicknames

What do you call family members besides their real names? (Not the ones when you're angry at them!) Do you call your daughter by her given name, or do you call her something like "Cookie" or "Peanut"? Do your kids call you Mom and Dad, or do they have special names for you? While pet names for parents are less common, pet names for kids are heard frequently and usually make them feel special.

The rest of the world may call your son "Justin," but calling him by his special, family-only name will give him a warm, family-only feeling.

Materials: None

Directions:

1. This normally isn't the sort of thing you sit down and consciously decide to do. ("Today I'm going to pick pet names for my kids.") Just be open to the possibility, and if something comes naturally to you, don't be afraid to use it. A pet name, as long as it's not something you tease the other person with, is another way of saying "I love you."

Helpful Hint: Make sure your kids are OK with the names you choose. Some kids are sensitive to anything but their real names.

Family Motto

While the motto on your Family Crest (page 36) will probably be only one word, you can also have a longer Family Motto. My mother's motto during my childhood was "moderation." She repeated it so often I accused her of being immoderate about it! Other families have longer sayings they've repeated so often that the sayings become de facto family mottoes.

Why not make it official? It might be a standard proverb such as "Anything worth doing is worth doing well," or "Never judge another person till you've walked a mile in their shoes," or some other phrase that people in your family use all the time.

Materials:
- White paper
- Pen or colored fine-line markers
- Glue
- Cardboard or corrugated cardboard
- Colored construction paper, glue, and scissors (optional)
- Material, needle, and threads suitable for needlepoint (optional)

Directions:
1. First, agree on your family motto. There might be some argument, so have everyone vote if necessary.

2. Print the motto neatly in the middle of a piece of white paper. Use fancy lettering if you like.

3. Draw a suitable design around the motto. You might want to cut a frame out of colored construction paper and glue it around the edges of the white paper. If you choose to include a frame, leave a blank border around the edge of the white paper where the frame will go.

4. Hang the finished motto on a suitable wall in the family room, hallway, kitchen, or another appropriate place.

5. You might choose to copy the motto and design it in needlepoint.

Helpful Hint: Make sure everyone participates in the construction of the finished product. Even the younger kids can cut and paste with adult supervision.

Family Song

If you spent your summers at camp, you may have been asked to take part in a "sing," which required your team to write and perform several songs. Typically, some of the funny songs in these "sings" were about life at camp. Let your kids write a funny song about your family. This activity is guaranteed to hit the hilarious notes of family life.

Materials:
- Paper and pen or pencil (for writing lyrics)
- Tape recorder and tape (optional)

Directions:
1. Think of significant events that have happened in the family such as the car breaking down the first time Bobby drove it after getting his license, or Kim getting her story published in the local paper. Also consider family occurrences that happen often and are worth poking gentle fun at, like Alissa using up all the hot water every time she washes her hair, or Mom's cakes always falling.

2. Think of popular or standard songs that are particularly appropriate to each topic you've selected. For example, if you've decided to write about how hard it is to get Will out of bed in the morning, "Reveille" would be an appropriate song. For a tune commemorating Chuck's tendency to serve nothing but soup when it's his turn to cook dinner, why not set your words to "The Campbells Are Coming."

3. Write your own lyrics to each song you've selected. The lyrics should humorously relate the family event you have chosen.

4. If you can't think of an appropriate tune for a particular event, use any tune.

5. Write as many verses as you can to as many different tunes as you need, commemorating as many of the family's foibles as possible.

6. Sing the song to the accompanying tune and record it on tape. Years from now, when you hear the tune "Everything's Coming Up Roses," you'll remember the verse you set to it and recall the time Nicole washed her new red shirt with Dad's underwear and left him wearing pink underpants for the rest of that year.

Helpful Hint: Help the younger kids select a tune to accompany their story. Also, help them write the words.

Limericks

You all know what a limerick looks like, right? These five-line poems are frequently known for their ribald content, but not all limericks are bawdy. Your family can have fun with each other by writing limericks that tease gently (and are as clean as a bar of Ivory soap). Please—no mean jibes. There's a big difference between laughing with people and laughing at them, or having fun with them and making fun of them.

Materials:
• Paper and pen or pencil

Directions:
1. Think of funny events or circumstances in your family. Does Rick spend all his time in front of the mirror worriedly checking for new pimples? Did Dad burn the steaks when he barbecued dinner for Mom's boss?

2. Write limericks to commemorate these events or circumstances. Keep it kind. Keep it funny.

3. The first, second, and fifth lines rhyme and usually have the following rhythm: da-da-DA-da-da-DA-da-da-DA. The third and fourth lines rhyme with a different sound and usually have the following rhythm: da-da-DA-da-da-DA. You can occasionally leave out one or more of the usual beats and still have a good limerick.

4. Work on the limericks together or have everyone work separately and compare results later.

5. Read the limericks aloud to each other or to family members who did not take part in their writing. See the following example:

> There once was a writer who dared
> To suggest that a family who cared
> Could poke gentle fun
> At this one and that one.
> Do you wonder how her family fared?

Helpful Hint: Read through a book of limericks to get into the spirit. You'll quickly acquire the sense of rhyme and rhythm needed for an effective limerick.

Secret Language

Most people know a little pig Latin, and there are numerous other secret languages. But what if your family had its own secret language? Wouldn't that make you kind of special and give you something that belongs to you and no one else? Then sit down with your family and think up a language all your own.

Materials: None

Directions:

1. Most secret languages, like ig-pay atin-Lay (pig Latin), are formed by adding an extra syllable to each word, by systematically moving a syllable, or by moving the initial sound of each word or syllable. But your secret language doesn't have to work that way. It can work any way you choose. First decide how you're going to create your secret language.

2. Teach the language technique to the rest of the family.

3. Practice a lot.

4. Don't explain the technique to anyone who isn't a family member. Your kids will enjoy being part of such a special—and secretive—family.

5. If any words from your secret language take root in normal language, write them down in the Family Dictionary (page 80).

Helpful Hint: A secret language can be tricky at first, but practice, practice, practice, and you'll eventually be quite good at speaking it.

Who Am I?

Parents want their kids to know a lot about their family, and kids enjoy having knowledge, especially when the learning is enjoyable. Who doesn't like to feel smart? But no child likes to feel as if she's in school when she's at home.

One game to promote family knowledge is "Who Am I?" In the original version, the name of a famous person is pinned to the back of each player. Players have to find out who they are by asking yes-or-no questions. In this family version of the game, a family member's name will be pinned to the back of each child.

Materials:
- Paper
- Pen or pencil
- Safety pins
- Scissors

Directions:
1. Cut out 2-inch-tall by 5-inch-wide strips of paper (they don't have to be exact). Give each player a piece of paper, a safety pin, and a pen or pencil.
2. Decide in advance who will be pinning a name on which player.
3. Each player writes the name of a family member on a sheet of paper. This includes extended family—aunts, uncles, cousins, grandparents, and so on—as well as immediate family. Then the player pins it to the back of another player. Nobody knows what name has been pinned on his or her own back, even though everyone can read the other players' names.
4. Players ask each other yes-or-no questions to try to figure out "who they are." Questions might include "Do I live in this house?" "Am I of our generation?" "Do I live in Chicago?" "Am I a guy?" "Do I own a pet skunk?" "Do I have four kids?" "Am I Aunt Marion?" and so on.
5. Decide how many chances each player will receive to guess his or her secret identity. For example, you could allow only one chance, and then the player is out of the game.

6. Here are four different sets of rules for asking questions. Some rules are more competitive than others. Choose which ones will work best for your family:

- Make sure everyone has an opportunity to ask at least one question. Then allow each player to guess her secret identity. If no one wants to guess, proceed to a second round of questioning. Each player who guesses correctly moves into a playoff round, but whoever guesses incorrectly is out of the game. It's all or nothing. Playoff players are given a new identity and the process is repeated until a winner is established.
- Each player asks one question at a time until everyone has either guessed right or guessed wrong. The player who guesses right with the fewest number of questions asked is the winner. Two or more players can win this way, if they all guess right on the same turn. Here, you can allow more than one chance to guess if you like.
- Each player asks five (or seven, or ten, or twelve) questions. If he can guess who he is within that number of questions, he's a winner (provided he hasn't made a wrong identification first). Theoretically, everyone can win.
- Each player gets to ask as many questions as she wants until she either guesses right or guesses wrong. If she guesses right, she's a winner. Again, everyone could win this way.

Helpful Hint: Give the younger kids more chances to guess their identities.

Trivial Pursuit, Family Version

Another game that promotes family knowledge and pride is a varia-
tion on Trivial Pursuit. For this, you'll need a Trivial Pursuit game
board and playing pieces, but instead of using the cards that came
with the game, you'll create your own cards. If one player creates all
the questions, then he won't be able to play, but if every family member contributes some of the cards, and if each player initials the cards
she contributed, then the whole family can play.

Materials:
- Trivial Pursuit game
- Index cards
- Pens

Directions:
1. Instead of the regular Trivial Pursuit categories, create your own.
   These will depend on your family size, the kids' knowledge of the
   extended family, and related factors. You might have categories
   such as Cousins, Pets, Ancestors, Occupations, Accomplishments,
   Family History, Milestones, Family Vacations, Family Summers,
   How Are We Related? and Where Do I Live? Color-code these categories to match the colors on the Trivial Pursuit game board.

2. Each player takes ten index cards (or more, if the kids are older)
   and writes a question with her initials on one side and the answer
   on the other. The questions should relate to the family and fit the
   categories you've chosen. Use these cards instead of the ones that
   came with the game.

3. To play, simply follow the rules of the regular game. If it's Kim's
   turn to receive a question and the top card bears her initials, then
   simply select the next card written by another player.

Helpful Hint: Help younger kids write questions that pertain to each
category if they are having trouble on their own.

Knowledge Chase

You don't need to have a Trivial Pursuit game (page 32) to play this family-knowledge game. Take any board game that involves moving pieces around a square or circle, add a few special ingredients, and you have everything you need for a fun game that will help the kids get to know their family history.

Materials:
- Any board game that offers a square or circular track with spaces to move through from start to finish
- Playing piece for each player
- Die
- Index cards and pens
- Stack of homemade cards with questions about the family

Directions:
1. Each player takes ten index cards (or more, if the kids are older) and writes a family question with his initials on one side and the answer on the other. Examples might include "What was the name of the summer camp Mom went to?" "Name Aunt Tina's old beagle," "What college did Nana graduate from?" "Name two merit badges Jeff has received," and so on.
2. Gather the cards and shuffle them thoroughly.
3. Everyone rolls the die once. The highest number goes first, with play proceeding clockwise from there.
4. Player one rolls the die, draws a card, and attempts to answer the question. If she selects one of her own questions, then she selects another card until she finds one written by another player.
5. If the player answers the question correctly, she moves forward the number of spaces rolled on the die. If she's wrong, she stays put.
6. Players get one turn at a time. Or, you could reward a correct answer with another turn.
7. The first player to travel the total number of spaces wins. You could require players to roll the exact number needed to land on the last space, or let them roll any number.

Helpful Hint: Help the younger kids by asking easier questions. You might make a special pile of cards just for them.

Secret Code

If your kids still don't get excited about learning family history, despite your best efforts to teach them, make the learning both fun and challenging by encoding the information. Have your kids try to decode their family history.

Materials:
• Paper and pens or pencils

Directions:
1. Create a key for encoding and decoding information. First, write the alphabet out in the usual order. Then, above or below each letter, write a different letter of the alphabet, which will stand for that letter in the encoded message. In a simple "step" code, you "step up" or "step down" the alphabet by one place (so that A = B, B = C, C = D, and so on). In a more challenging step code, you could go up or down the alphabet by several steps (for example, A = G, B = H, C = I, and so on). In a random code, there is no regular system for assigning letters, but be sure you use each code letter only once.

2. After you've selected a key, use it to encode bits of family information such as "Grandpa Arthur came to Des Moines from Canada when he was seven years old," "Aunt Iris once worked in a fireworks factory," "Mom's first dog was named Patches," and so on. Carefully proofread your work.

3. Give the key and the encoded messages to your kids.

4. Simply decoding "secret information" should be fun enough for them, but you can raise the interest level further by offering a modest prize to the child who correctly decodes the message first.

5. For older kids, or kids who like a serious challenge, you can provide messages without the key, so they must figure out the code before they decipher the message. You can decode one word for them as a hint, if you like.

Helpful Hint: Don't make the codes so difficult that the kids get bored. Remember, the object is to have fun while learning about the family.

Crafting Family Traditions

Family Crest or Coat of Arms

A family crest shows pride in your family's history and values. For centuries, kings, knights, and other nobility have proudly displayed their family crests on their flags, shields, and castles. You may not own a castle, but you can still design a family crest for your noble family. You can use it in a variety of fun ways.

Materials:
- Paper
- Fine-line markers or colored pencils (optional)

Directions:
1. Choose a short motto to put on the crest. It should be something that's important to your family such as "Truth" or "Try Harder."

2. Select a few pictures for the crest. The pictures should illustrate items that are important to your family. Did Grandpa make the family fortune in his factory? Show the smokestacks. Is the family crazy about animals? Show your pets. Is your garden the show-place of the neighborhood? Show your vegetables.

3. Draw a crest or shield shape. Divide it into sections for the pictures and motto. Write the motto and draw the pictures in the appropriate spaces. Here are three sample formats: (a) One picture takes up the entire crest except for the bottom, where you write the motto; (b) Divide the crest into four sections, putting the motto in one section and a picture in each of the other three sections; (c) Divide the crest into five sections: four squares and a strip either at the top or in the middle. The motto goes in the strip, and pictures go in the four squares.

4. You might use the crest in one of the following ways: Hang it in your hallway or family room, scan it into your computer to use as a screen saver, display it on the cover of a Family Cookbook (pages 14 and 15) or Family History (page 12), use it on Family Stationery (page 48), include it on the Family Flag (page 37), or paint it on your Family Mailbox (page 46).

Helpful Hint: Have the kids vote on what the motto should be, and also have them draw pictures to illustrate the crest.

Family Flag

Every country has a flag it displays as a symbol of national pride. Why shouldn't your family have one, too? Your family flag might incorporate the Family Crest or Coat of Arms (page 36), family colors, drawings of family members, and so on. Hang your flag at the front of the house or any other place that seems appropriate.

Materials:
- Large, rectangular piece of white canvas
- Permanent, colored, fine-line markers
- Glue
- Large, sturdy pole such as a broomstick or mop handle

Directions:
1. Have every family member sketch a design for a flag, then get together and compare ideas, selecting the best ones and incorporating them into the final design.
2. If you have one particularly talented family member, ask him to create the flag by drawing on both sides of a piece of white canvas. Use the colors and design the family has agreed on.
3. Glue the edge of the flag to a pole such as a broomstick or mop handle.
4. Display the flag by sticking the broomstick into the ground or using a flag holder to secure the broomstick.

Helpful Hint: Everybody can contribute to this project. Have the contributions incorporated into a collage by a preselected designer.

Family Totem Pole

Totem poles originated more than two hundred years ago among the Native American coastal cultures in what is now British Columbia and Alaska. Among these cultures, the connection between the animals depicted on a totem pole and the family to which the pole pertains is very important. Your family's totem pole can continue this tradition of family symbolism and pride. Locate your totem pole in a prominent place in your house.

Materials:
- One oatmeal or Saltines box, or any cylindrical container, for each family member (Be sure everyone uses the same type.)
- Glue, construction paper, fine-line markers, crayons, paints
- Family photos, feathers, shells, and other decorative objects (optional)

Directions:
1. Each family member decorates his or her box according to individual taste. The final product should be an expression of that family member's character and personality. You may want to follow the Northwest Native American traditions, which use an animal as the mystical totem spirit for each person. For example, you might embrace the diligence of the beaver, the friendliness and loyalty of the dog, and the strength of the horse or bear.

2. Decoration options are virtually unlimited. For example, you could draw pictures on paper and glue these onto the boxes; glue photos to the paper or directly to the box; create cardboard or construction paper wings to extend from the box; or create cardboard or construction-paper facial features to be similarly glued onto the box. Use your imagination.

3. Weight the bottom box with rocks or other heavy objects to lend stability to the totem pole. Sand works, too, but is more likely to create a mess if it seeps out.

4. Arrange the decorated boxes in a stack and glue them together.

5. If you wish, use strips of construction paper to cover the seams and add colorful stripes to the overall design.

Helpful Hint: Make sure to seal the boxes securely when constructing the pole, to prevent them from toppling and injuring someone.

Symbolic Family Quilt

Though quilting is an art that takes considerable skill, you can make a beautiful and symbolic quilt without being a master quilter. This quick-and-easy quilt project is perfect for kids, and the finished product will be a lovely accent that can be used as a bedcover, wall hanging, or table runner.

Materials:
- Towel, bedsheet, or similar sheet of fabric to use for backing (the size will depend on how you intend to use the quilt.)
- Fabrics in many colors
- Scissors
- Needle and thread

Directions:
1. Work together to design your family quilt. You might want to reproduce the design on your family flag or crest, or you might want to use the same colors to create a different design.
2. Cut the fabric into strips, circles, squares, or whatever shapes are required to create the intended design.
3. Arrange the cut fabric onto the backing fabric so it resembles the intended design.
4. Sew the fabric onto the backing. For a wall hanging or runner, towels or cut portions of a large sheet will do. If you're cutting a piece of a sheet, hem the frayed edges before you sew the cut fabric pieces to it. If you want your quilt to serve as a bedcover, you'll need a complete sheet or similar-sized fabric as a backing.

Helpful Hint: Carefully supervise children who have been allowed to use needles.

Nostalgic Family Quilt

Some quilts feature traditional designs, while others capture important family moments. Unlike the Symbolic Family Quilt (page 39), the Nostalgic Family Quilt preserves images from some of your family's most cherished times together. Even though this quilt takes time to create, it will safeguard precious memories for several lifetimes.

Materials:
- Old shirts and sweatshirts with meaningful logos or designs such as old school shirts or souvenir shirts from family trips
- Pieces of fabric or old clothing that contain patterns meaningful to your family
- Scissors
- Needles and thread
- Towel, dishtowel, or bedsheet, depending on the size of quilt desired

Directions:
1. Carefully cut around the designs, words, or logos that you want to preserve from old T-shirts or sweatshirts. Cut similar-sized swatches of fabric from other meaningful garments.

2. Arrange and rearrange the various cut pieces on your backing fabric until you've found a pleasing design.

3. Sew the cut pieces onto the backing. If necessary, consult a quilt book at your local library or bookstore to learn various styles of stitching you might use.

4. If you're using the quilt as a wall hanging, you may wish to frame it.

Helpful Hint: Carefully supervise children who have been allowed to use needles.

Family Shirts

You've seen families that have had print shops or silk-screen businesses make special family T-shirts or sweatshirts. Usually they say something like "Schmidt Family Reunion, July 2000." But there's no reason to wait for a big event to make a family shirt. This fun activity will enable your kids to show their family pride wherever they go.

Materials:
- A sweatshirt, T-shirt, or turtleneck for each member of the family
- Fabric in many colors
- Needles and thread
- Scissors

Directions:
1. Decide on a design for your shirts. Try to coordinate the shirts with the colors in your family flag or crest. You can also spell out words such as "Sanford Family" across the front of the shirts.
2. Cut out strips of fabric and sew them onto the shirts according to the design you've selected. This sewing time will be a great opportunity to share memories.
3. You might also consider using colorful fabric paints to create designs on everyone's shirts.
4. Wear your shirts with pride.

Helpful Hint: Carefully supervise children who have been allowed to use needles.

Family Caps

Now that you have a Family Shirt (page 41), you can't wear just any old cap with it! You need a special cap that matches the shirt. Wear your matching outfits with pride!

Materials:
- Plain baseball cap for each family member
- Permanent fine-line markers or fancy fabric paint
- Souvenir pins and buttons

Directions:
1. Select an inexpensive baseball cap for each member of the family. You might prefer the lightest, most neutral color so that the markings will show up easily.

2. Have each family member use markers to decorate the upper surface of his cap's bill in a unique way. Each person chooses his own design, but all should work with the same colors. Ideally, colors should be the same as those used on the Family Shirts (page 41). The design should include the first name of the family member.

3. If you've chosen fabric paint, follow the instructions that come with the paint, and be sure to let it dry thoroughly before wearing the cap!

4. In an arch shape on the back of the cap, inscribe the family name.

5. As the years go by, family members can add further personal meaning to their caps by decorating them with souvenirs the family acquires on vacation, at the county fair, and during other activities. The end result will be special caps that symbolize family pride and express the individuality and personal experiences of each family member.

Helpful Hint: Don't forget to take your cap on family vacation!

Family Calendar

A family calendar shows important dates that involve one or more members of the family. It will help you plan and organize your activities, and it will be fun to make!

Materials:
- Twelve sheets of construction paper
- Hole punch, pencil, ruler, glue
- Two 1-foot lengths of yarn
- Fine-line markers or colored pencils
- Hooks to hang the calendar

Directions:
1. Hold a piece of construction paper sideways. Punch two holes at what is now the top (the long side of the paper). Each hole should be approximately one-third of the way in from each side.

2. Using that piece of paper as a guide, punch holes in the same place on each of the other sheets.

3. Keeping the holes at the top of each page, draw a calendar grid on each page. Use a ruler to get a straight line, and draw with marker or colored pencil.

4. Write the month above the grid and fill in the numbers in the appropriate squares. Use a commercial calendar as a guide, so you know which day of the week each month starts on. You may want to use a different-colored pencil or marker for each month.

6. Draw a little picture on each page.

7. Make sure you have the pages in order. Jog them so the holes are lined up. Loop a piece of yarn through the left-hand holes and loop another through the right-hand holes. Knot the loops. The loops should be large enough so that the pages turn easily. There should be plenty of room to use the loops to hang the calendar.

8. Write all regularly occurring events on the calendar, using ordinary pencil so they can be erased in case things change. As family members schedule other plans, write those in, too.

9. Hang the calendar.

Helpful Hint: Have the kids draw pictures on each calendar page.

Individual Calendar

Each member of the family may want to have a special calendar in his or her room. You can accommodate everyone by simply following the instructions for making a Family Calendar (page 43), or you can use this shortcut.

Materials:
- A free commercial calendar from your bank, insurance agent, or employer
- Thirteen sheets of white construction paper (typing paper is too thin), or one sheet of white or pale construction paper and twelve horizontal pictures
- Paints, crayons, or colored fine-line markers
- Glue or double-faced poster tape
- Hole punch

Directions:
1. Draw a horizontal cover for the calendar. It might say something like "Danny Delafield's Calendar" or "2001 by Sue Newton." Make sure to include some kind of picture or design.

2. Attach the picture to the front of the calendar, on top of the calendar's original cover. Glue or tape it in place.

3. If you don't have twelve horizontal pictures that you really like, draw as many as you need to make a total of twelve.

4. Attach each picture over one of the twelve pictures already in the calendar, using glue or double-faced tape.

5. Line up a hole punch with the hole in each page and punch through your newly pasted picture so you'll be able to hang the calendar.

6. List all your important dates on that calendar. Start by filling in family members' birthdays, parents' and grandparents' anniversaries, and other significant dates. Later you can fill in everything from dental appointments to dates with friends and family trips to friends' birthday parties.

Helpful Hint: Hang your calendar in a prominent place: near your bedroom, in the kitchen, in the playroom—anyplace with high visibility.

Birthday Calendar

"Patti, did you remember to send a birthday card to Grandpa?"
"When's his birthday?"

You might be familiar with this conversation. A good way to avoid a last-minute rush to the card shop is to make sure Patti knows about birthdays in plenty of time to send cards. She should have a calendar showing the birthdays of everyone in the family (and anniversaries, and other regularly celebrated occasions). This can be a store-bought calendar, a freebie from your insurance agent, or a calendar your kids draw themselves.

Your kids like getting cards on their birthdays. Cousin Jodi, Uncle Joe, and Grandma Ivy are no different—and now your kids will have no reason to forget to send them cards.

Materials:
• Calendar (homemade or commercial)
• Pen

Directions:
1. Encourage your child to make a homemade calendar if you don't have a freebie and don't want to buy one from the store.
2. Provide all your family members' birth dates, anniversaries, and other significant occasions. Have your child write the dates in the appropriate date boxes on the calendar.
3. Remind your child to look at the calendar regularly to see what family occasions are coming up, and to make or buy a card for each occasion. Encourage her to send it out in plenty of time.
4. Your child might want to include her friends' birthdays, too.

Helpful Hint: A calendar can be personalized with painted pictures, sketches, poems, and so on. It's a great way to get used to calendars if you're not currently a calendar person.

Family Mailbox

How often do notes from school, important mail, and other papers go astray? Create a Family Mailbox so everyone will always know where to look for those V.I.P.s—Very Important Papers!

Materials:
- One shoebox with the lid removed for each family member
- Different-colored paints (be sure to include either white or another pale color) and a paintbrush
- Newspapers (to protect your work surface)

Directions:
1. Spread out newspaper to protect your work surface.
2. Use one shoebox for each family member. Remove the lid from the shoebox.
3. Paint the outside of the shoebox with white or a pale-colored paint. You might want to paint the inside of the shoebox, too.
4. At one end of each shoebox, paint a family member's name to designate that person's mailbox.
5. Paint a design or picture on the other three sides of the shoebox, and perhaps on the end where the name is, too.
6. When the shoeboxes are dry, place them in a central location such as the kitchen counter, a table in the entry hall, or on a shelf in the family room.
7. If you have mail, a message, or anything else for another family member, put it in that person's shoebox. Now everyone knows where to look for mail, messages from family members, phone messages, notes, and other important stuff.

Helpful Hint: Encourage each child to paint his or her own shoebox.

Family Message Center

Along with the family mailbox, you can create a message center to improve communication between family members. Phone numbers, memos, grocery lists—everyone will know where to put and look for family messages.

Materials:
- A 2-by-1-foot piece of corkboard
- Pushpins, scissors, hammer, nails, pen or pencil
- Bright, colorful yarn as long and wide as your corkboard (Multiply the length of the yarn by the number of family members. This means that a 2-foot corkboard in a family of four would call for 8 feet of yarn.)
- Colorful marking pens
- A pad of 3-by-5-inch paper

Directions:
1. Nail the corkboard to a wall.

2. Cut the yarn into lengths as long (or wide) as the corkboard. Cut as many lengths of yarn as there are members of the family.

3. Divide the corkboard into roughly equal sections, one for each member of the family and one for the whole family. Do this by tacking the yarn in straight lines across or down the corkboard, using pushpins, until you have created the necessary number of sections on the corkboard.

4. Create a name tag for each person's section and one for the entire family. Use one piece of 3-by-5-inch paper for each name tag. Let each family member draw his own name tag and decorate it as he wishes. Tack the tag at the top or left side of the appropriate section.

5. Leave the pad of paper and a pen or pencil as close to the message center as possible. Also, leave plenty of unused pushpins pushed securely into empty sections of the corkboard.

6. As each family member needs to leave a message for another, she writes it on a piece of paper from the pad and sticks it in that person's section of the corkboard. Phone messages can go on the corkboard message center, too.

Helpful Hint: Locate the message center in a high-traffic place.

Family Stationery

There's nothing like personalized stationery to add a touch of pride to your outgoing mail. Family stationery can contain the names of everyone in your family—making it perfect for correspondence with relatives and friends. Best of all, you don't need to pay a small fortune to have this stationery printed.

If you have a computer and scanner, you can create family stationery right on your computer. But if you're not in a position to do this, or want to spend some quality family time creating personalized stationery the old-fashioned way, this project is perfect for you.

Materials:
- One sheet of 8½-by-11-inch white paper
- Black or dark blue pen, glue
- Typewriter, computer, photocopier (optional)

Directions:
1. First create your original piece of stationery. Type your family's name and address at the top of a sheet of typing paper. You'll probably want to center this information, which is easier with a computer but can be managed with a typewriter, too. You may want to list every family member's name.

2. If you like, you can add your family motto underneath your address or off to one side.

3. You can also include your Family Crest or Coat of Arms (page 36), either off to one side again or above your name. You can draw it directly on the stationery, or you can make a photocopy of it and glue that onto the stationery.

4. After completing the original piece of stationery, make copies by either photocopying the sheet or by taking it to a commercial printer. Consider making the copies on colored paper rather than plain white —perhaps a distinguished ivory or a pale blue.

5. Now, whenever a family member writes a letter to a friend or relative, she can use the family stationery to demonstrate her family pride.

Helpful Hint: Some copy centers have computers on-site that you can use for a small fee.

Family Address Book

Keep all those important addresses and phone numbers in a family address book. Does Tommy need Aunt Claire's address so he can send a thank-you note? Does Mom need the address of Marcia's friend Ellyn so she knows where to pick up her daughter on Wednesday? Does Paige need to call the library? All of this information can be right at your fingertips in this simple family project.

Materials:
- Small loose-leaf notebook
- Filler paper (the right size for the notebook)
- Alphabetical divider tags
- Bright-colored marking pen
- Pen

Directions:
1. Using a bright-colored marking pen, write your family's name and "Address and Phone Book" on the notebook cover.
2. Attach an alphabetical divider tab to each of twenty-six pages and insert these into the book.
3. Place at least a few sheets of blank paper behind each divider page.
4. Fill in names, phone numbers, addresses, and other important information on each page. You can probably fit two to four listings on each page, depending on the size of notebook you bought, how large you write, and how much information you fill in for each person.
5. You might want to include other information besides an address and phone number. For your kids' friends, you might want to know which of your kids they "belong" to, as well as their parents' names. For businesses and libraries, you might want the hours these places are open.
6. You might want to alphabetize your kids' friends' names by their first names. You might also want to list the dentist and doctor under "D." This is particularly useful for the babysitter, who might need to find the doctor's number and not know his or her name. Similarly, Grandma could go under "G" and so on.

Helpful Hint: As information in the book gets outdated, you can discard the pages that are no longer needed and add new ones.

Art Gallery

Your kids have undoubtedly created lots of priceless art over the years: drawings, finger paintings, compositions, poems, and so on. You can't hang them all on the walls, but you can show off the ones that are extraspecial.

Start an art gallery in your hallway! If you have a hallway alongside a stairway, or one that leads from your kitchen to your living room, or one that runs from bedroom to bedroom, you have a perfect gallery for displaying your family's artistic treasures.

Materials:
- Artwork, original stories, school compositions, and whatever else you want to display
- Removable, double-faced poster tape

Directions:
1. It might be best to let the parents make the decisions about what art are should be displayed and where, so there's no fighting about this among the kids.
2. Attach a strip of removable, double-faced poster tape in each corner of the pieces and hang them on the wall.
3. Replace one artwork with another whenever you wish.

Helpful Hint: You could have each kid select a few favorite pieces, but make sure everyone is represented fairly.

Photo Collage

Here's one way to have fun with family photos. This project is also perfect for kids who have relatives they don't see very often. Your kids will become more familiar with their extended family while making this photo collage.

Materials:
• Cardboard (at least 8½ by 11 inches, and larger is better)
• Construction paper
• Glue
• Photos
• Scissors
• Optional: Bits of gift wrap, lace, ribbons, glitter, and a copy of your Family Crest or Coat of Arms (page 36)

Directions:

1. Glue construction paper over the cardboard.

2. Cut out photos of family members—faces only or full bodies, depending on the layout you intend. Make sure the photos are copies. (You obviously don't want to ruin the originals.)

3. Arrange the cut photos of relatives artfully on the construction paper. Play with the arrangement until you're happy with it. Photos can overlap in some cases, if you like.

4. Glue the photos in place once you've decided on an arrangement.

5. Add ribbons, lace, other materials, and glitter to the collage (optional).

6. If you've created a Family Crest or Coat of Arms, include a copy of that in the collage, too (optional).

Helpful Hint: As you help your kids with this project, be sure to tell them stories about the different relatives in the photos.

Assemble a Photo Album

If you're family is like most, you have shoeboxes full of photos stuffed into a closet somewhere. You probably think that you'll always remember why Caitlin was wearing that sunflower costume in the photograph taken in front of Monica's house, or why Brian was dressed in a suit in the photo taken in his bedroom. But you might be surprised when, after a few years, no one can recall the stories behind these pictures.

It's time to assemble a photo album—one that will not only preserve the pictures but will also contain enough information to jog your memory on the details of the photos. Best of all, a photo album is easier to flip through than a shoebox!

Materials:
- Photo album(s)
- Photos, Paper, Pen, Scissors, Glue

Directions:
1. Organize the photos. If your family takes lots of pictures, you may want an album for each child, one for the parents, one for the whole family, and one for other relatives. You might also want to organize photos chronologically or by subjects such as school, camp, holidays, and so on.

2. Place each photo in its place on an album page. Leave room below the photo for a piece of paper that explains the circumstances of the picture.

3. Create a label for each photo. You should include at least names, dates, and places.

4. Place the labels under the photos, using glue if you don't have a self-stick album.

5. To provide even greater detail about the photos, put a number under each photo and write the information about the picture in a photo guide. Write the number on the back of the photo, too.

Helpful Hint: A monthly photo album night is a great way to record new family history and to preserve precious memories. Once a month or so, gather to paste new pictures you've accumulated and to look at pictures from previous albums.

Decorate Your Mailbox

Communicate your family's individuality with a mailbox unlike any other on the block. Lots of people have their names or house numbers on their mailboxes, but your family can show its special pride and creativity with this fun project!

Materials:
- Standard metal curbside or porch-style mailbox (Plastic ones won't hold paint very well.)
- Can of spray-style primer (Rustoleum is good.)
- Latex or oil-based paints
- Paintbrushes
- Turpentine and rags for cleanup

Directions:
1. Prepare the mailbox at least a few hours in advance by covering the outer surfaces with a coat of spray-on primer. Depending on local climate, the primer should take only an hour or two to dry. However, it's a good idea to give the primer a full day to dry before decorating.

2. Agree on a design that will illustrate your family's individuality and pride. You may want to paint the Family Flag (page 37), the Family Coat of Arms (page 36), a fancy version of the first initial of your family's name, or some picture that displays the family's interests (boats, horses, or cats, for example). You may even want to paint the Family Motto (page 26).

3. Paint the design on the mailbox.

4. Don't mount your new mailbox outdoors until the paint is dry. Depending on the colors and paint that you've used, it could take anywhere from a couple of days to a week or more before the mailbox is completely dried.

Helpful Hint: Follow the paint instructions and carefully supervise the younger kids, especially with oil-based paint.

Family Birdhouse Sign

Historians refer to the families of kings and queens as "The House of Windsor," or "The House of Hapsburg." Why not announce your home with a striking sign that says "The House of Soriano"? These signs are both practical and decorative, they're easy to make, and they can be a terrific expression of your family's individuality. This particular sign will also demonstrate your family's clever creativity, since your sign will be in the form of a cute birdhouse!

Materials:
- ¼-inch or ½-inch plywood about 1 foot wide and 18 inches to 2 feet tall
- Paint or fine-line markers
- Small scraps of wood, bark, or shingle, or a 16- to 20-inch piece of balsa, molding, or other thin wood roughly 2 inches wide
- Glue or glue gun
- Light colored varnish, stain, or paint
- Moss, dried flowers, 1-inch length of ¼-inch dowel, and other decorative items as inspiration suggests (optional)

Directions:
1. Design your birdhouse on paper, selecting both geometry and dimensions that appeal to you. Cut plywood to match the major pieces of the birdhouse. One design option follows: Cut two equal-sized square pieces (the front and back of the house) and three equal-sized rectangular pieces (the sides and floor of the house). For the roof, cut a measured piece of plywood in half. Cut the ends at 45-degree angles so they will fit against each other and the sides. The angled pieces will join together to form the peaked roof. You can also add shingles or a piece of bark to create a more rustic roof.

2. Before assembling the pieces, sand the wood until it's fairly smooth.

3. Glue the pieces together. Use small nails if necessary for stability. Drill a 1-inch hole slightly above the center of the house. Then drill a ¼-inch hole 1 inch below that hole. Insert a 2-inch length of dowel into the smaller hole, making a bird perch.

4. Stain, varnish, or paint the house. While the paint is drying, decide on decorations that will make the sign distinctly your own. Perhaps your family identifies with a particular bird—woodpeckers because you're determined, hawks because you're dedicated hunters, doves because you work for peace, or nuthatches because sometimes that's what your family seems like!

5. Once the surface is dry, decorate the sign according to your design. Paint a picture of a bird, your family's initial, or your Family Flag (page 37) or Crest (page 36). Or paint a picture of something associated with your family's interests—sports equipment, books, or whatever seems appropriate. Beyond painting, you can decorate your birdhouse with moss, bark, or dried flowers. Use whatever accents you want to create a sign that tells people why you're a proud family.

Helpful Hint: Make sure to carefully supervise younger kids around power tools.

Place Mats

With this project, each family member can have a place mat that is both unique and clearly part of a family set. Best of all, your kids will have fun making their own place mats.

Materials for each mat:
- One sheet of 8-by-12-inch drawing paper (or heavyweight typing paper)
- Crayons or colored fine-line markers, scissors
- Clear contact paper (18 inches wide)

Directions:
1. Agree on a general design for the place mats.

2. Have everyone draw his own place mat to match the general design that's been selected, but allow each family member to use his own imagination when it comes to drawing the picture on the place mat. Be sure to make one that says "Guest."

3. Cut two 18-by-10-inch pieces of contact paper, leaving the backing on.

4. Place one of these pieces flat on the table, backing-side up, and carefully remove the backing.

5. Center the drawing above the adhesive, design-side down. Carefully place the drawing on the adhesive paper, pressing from center to edges to eliminate air bubbles or wrinkles.

6. Place the second piece of adhesive paper, backing-side up, on the table, and remove the backing. Carefully place the first piece—with the drawing on it—on top of this, so that the back of the drawing is facing the adhesive.

7. Having sandwiched the drawing between the two pieces of adhesive paper, repeat the smoothing process with the second sheet of adhesive paper, pressing from center to edges to eliminate air bubbles or wrinkles.

8. With scissors, trim away the excess adhesive paper carefully, leaving a one-inch border of adhesive paper around the drawing.

Helpful Hint: Incorporate your Family Crest or Coat of Arms (page 36), Flag (page 37), or any other special family items.

Decorate a Tablecloth

Your family can create a tablecloth that's uniquely your own. The tablecloth can be for picnics, informal holidays, or everyday. Regardless of the occasion, it will be unlike any other tablecloth.

Materials:
- Solid-colored full sheet (white or pastel)
- Permanent fine-line color markers
- Newspapers and plastic trash bags
- Masking tape

Directions:

1. Decide on a format for the tablecloth:

   - Will you use the Family Coat of Arms (page 36), Family Motto (page 26), Family Flag (page 37), or all of the above?
   - Will you divide the tablecloth into sections and have each child— or each family member—draw in his or her section? Will you have each family member sign his or her name? Or will you have the semi-official family artist do all the drawing?
   - Is everyone allowed to use any color he wants, or will you limit the tablecloth to colors that blend harmoniously with your dining room paint or wallpaper?

2. Spread several layers of newspaper and plastic trash bags on the floor to prevent the paint from bleeding through and staining. Place the sheet on top of the newspapers and secure it firmly to the floor with masking tape.

3. Have everyone (or just the family artist) start decorating the sheet. If the tablecloth is to be used for holidays, birthdays, or some other occasion, an appropriate drawing is necessary. Otherwise, a general design, such as the Family Crest, is best.

Helpful Hint: For kids too young to sign their names, you can trace their hands or let them draw a picture. Then you can write their names for them.

Family Napkin Rings

Even simple, practical items like napkin rings can express both family pride and individuality. Some families prefer each member's napkin ring to be different from the others so there's never any doubt about ownership. Other families prefer their napkin rings to be a uniform set. Try to choose designs that symbolize your family. An interesting napkin-ring design can stimulate dinner discussions about various family traits or stories represented by the drawings.

Materials:
- Undecorated wood napkin rings from a craft store (or heavy cardboard tubing from rolls of wrapping paper or paper towels)
- X-acto knife if using cardboard
- Acrylic paints and small brushes (or fine-line markers)

Directions:
1. Decide on a design for the rings. Will you use names, initials, the last initial only, a design, or some combination of these? Does your family have a special color, Flag (page 37), Motto (page 26), Crest (page 36), or byword? If so, you can incorporate these into the design. Decide if all the rings will be uniform or individualized.

2. If using cardboard tubing, cut napkin-ring-sized circles about 1½ inches wide.

3. If using cardboard, paint or color a uniform background color with a marking pen on the entire outer side of the napkin ring (and the inner side if you like). Off-white or light tan would work well. You may also choose to do this with wood, but it isn't necessary.

4. Paint or draw the design on each ring (name, initial, flower, and so on). Allow time to dry.

Helpful Hint: Cutting the cardboard can be dangerous, so supervise the younger ones and delegate tasks as you see fit.

Family-Design Seed Centerpiece

Any centerpiece can add class to your dining room table. What makes a family centerpiece special is that it symbolizes something unique about the family that's eating dinner together.

Materials:
- Four pieces of ¼-inch plywood or heavy cardboard, cut into oblong shapes roughly 6 to 7 inches long and 4 inches high
- Glue
- An assortment of seeds and grains such as lentils, split peas, barley, rice, sunflower seeds, corn, brown rice, sesame seeds, peppercorns, or a sampling from a bag of mixed birdseed (The specific types don't matter as long as you have an assortment of colors, sizes, and textures.)
- Small corner braces and screws, or duct tape or strapping tape
- Vase or jar filled with dried, fresh, or artificial flowers

Directions:
1. Sketch your Family Crest (page 36), Flag (page 37), Motto (page 26), name, or other symbolic design on each of the pieces of plywood or cardboard.

2. Establish four groups of family members and have each create a seed mosaic of the design by gluing seeds of various colors and textures to the flat surfaces of the wood or cardboard. Have each group spread white glue over only a small area at a time. Then cover the glue with seeds or grains. You'll end up with four panels that match in design yet are unique in color and appearance.

3. Fasten the panels together so they form a box—four walls without a bottom or top.

4. Put this box in the center of the table.

5. Fill the box with flowers to grace your table.

Helpful Hint: You might want to pencil-sketch the design on the plywood or cardboard first, before gluing seeds and grains.

Glowing Family Centerpiece

You can make a glowing centerpiece for your dinner table using a setup similar to the one found in Family Votive Lights (page 61).

Materials:
- One large glass votive candle holder and candle
- Plain white typing paper
- Pen, fine-line markers, glue (not rubber cement or tape)

Directions:

1. Cut a strip of typing paper long enough to wrap once around the candle holder and ½ inch smaller in width than the height of the candle holder.

2. On the paper, draw the Family Crest (page 36), Flag (page 37), or whatever you want to display. Draw it tall enough to fill most of the height of the paper. Color it with a marker. (Don't use crayon.)

3. Glue the paper strip to the candle holder. Make sure the paper does not stick up above the top edge of the glass!

4. Light the candle. The Flag or Crest will glow, backlighted, gracing your dinner table.

Important: Carefully observe these precautions with votive candles:
- Do not place the candles in a position that might cause anything above them to ignite.
- Do not place the candles near the edge of the table where they might slide off, come in contact with a little one reaching for the mashed potatoes, or be bumped off by vibrations, kids, or pets.
- Make sure your kids avoid touching, playing with, or allowing anything to get near the flame.
- Remind the kids that a candle holder can get very hot while the candle burns, so touching the glass is a no-no.
- Do not place the candle within reach of very young kids.
- Place a trivet, plate, or other heat-safe object under the candle to protect your table, tablecloth, and place mats.
- Do not leave the candles unattended after the meal is finished.

Helpful Hint: If you have a rambunctious child, you may want to skip this craft!

Family Votive Lights

How about having your family name in lights? Your family name or Motto (page 26) can be proudly displayed on a mantelpiece, bookshelf, windowsill, or other prominent surface with Family Votive Lights.

Materials:
- One small glass votive candle and holder for each letter of your family name or Motto
- Plain white typing paper
- Pen
- Felt-tip, fine-line markers
- Glue (not rubber cement or tape)

Directions:
1. Cut a strip of typing paper long enough to wrap once around the votive candle holder, and about one-half inch smaller in width than the height of the candle holder. Make one strip for each letter of the family name or Motto—in other words, one for each candle holder.

2. With a pen, outline one letter of the family name on each paper strip. Try to make the letters the same size, and make them tall enough so that they fill most of the height of the paper. Color each letter with a marker. (Don't use crayon.) You may want to color all the letters the same, make each letter a different solid color, or decorate the letters in different and fanciful ways.

3. Glue the paper strips to the candle holders. Make sure the paper does not stick up above the top edge of the glass!

4. Arrange the candles so they spell the family name or Motto.

5. Light the candle. The letters of the family name will glow, back-lighted and beautiful, a warm expression of your family's unity and pride.

Helpful Hint: Carefully observe the precautions about votive candles on page 60.

"Time to Grow" Clock

A "Time to Grow" clock doesn't tell the time at all—but it sure shows how time is passing and how the kids in your family are growing. Make one "clock" for each child in the family.

Materials:
- Cardboard (or wood and a jigsaw)
- Scissors, glue, photos
- Permanent fine-line marker (or paint and paintbrush)

Directions:
1. Cut out a fairly large clock face from cardboard (or make a more durable one out of wood).

2. Paint small hour numbers in the usual positions on the clock face, using paint on wood and either paint or permanent marker on cardboard.

3. On each child's clock near the number 1, paste your child's picture as he appeared in first grade. Adjacent to the number 2, paste the child's second-grade picture, and so on. Continue to add pictures over the years through "twelve o'clock"—senior year of high school.

4. You could make the pasting of each year's picture a ceremonial occasion that is solemn, festive, or somewhere in between:
   - Have each child say how she thinks she's grown as a person— not just in height or size—since the last picture was pasted, and what she would like to accomplish in the year to come.
   - Toast the milestone with a festive drink, and wear party hats.
   - Host a special dinner in your kid's honor, and have him plan the menu (with reasonable choices, of course).
   - Enjoy any other ceremony with accents like candles, singing, special foods or beverages, fancy table settings or very informal ones, promises for self-improvement, prayers of thanksgiving, stories about the past year, or other special ways to mark the child's physical growth or emotional or spiritual progress.

Helpful Hint: Have the kids help choose a ceremony and select the photos that will appear on the clock faces.

Family Pastimes

Family Dinner Night

If on most nights your family has at least one member absent from the dinner table, you should consider establishing one night of the week when dinner attendance is sacred. Sunday is probably the best option—the night when Mom and Dad are least likely to have a business or parental commitment, and when none of the kids is likely to have band, volleyball, Scouts, a sleepover, and so on.

Make it a rule that everyone needs to be there—and everyone means everyone. "There" means at the table—not in front of the TV or at a desk doing last-minute homework.

Materials:
- One night designated Family Dinner Night
- The Family Journal (page 6), Scrapbook (page 7), Photo Album (page 52), or other related items

Directions:
1. If you normally eat at the dining room table, this may be your night to eat informally in the kitchen. Or, if you normally eat in the kitchen or breakfast nook, this may be your night to eat at the dining room table.
2. You could make this the kids' night to cook, if they're old enough, or it could be a request night, when the children take turns choosing the menu (within reason) from one week to the next. Or this could be Family Heirloom Recipe Night (page 14).
3. After dinner, you could have some other activity that becomes a tradition. This might be a family discussion, a formal debate on current affairs, a look through the Family Journal at the entries for this week last year, a look through old photo albums or scrapbooks, or a Family Council meeting (page 65).

Helpful Hint: Remember, Family Dinner should be special—and fun. Having everyone together should be cherished by your kids, so emphasize the importance of being together while downplaying the obligation.

Family Council Meeting

While family meetings vary from family to family, at minimum they are gatherings where family members discuss items of interest or importance to most or all present. Where should we go on the family vacation? What should we eat for the next Family Dinner Night (page 64)? Who's going to cut the grass this summer? These questions can be addressed in a Family Council Meeting.

Materials: None

Directions:

1. Establish a specific time every week for a Family Council Meeting. If you have a regularly scheduled Family Dinner Night, a good time to have the meeting is directly after dinner.

2. Any family member can make any announcement of general interest at the meeting. This can include anything from announcing Joni's forthcoming dance recital to news that Mom is pregnant.

3. If a sibling thinks Bobby should be doing more around the house, or if Sara thinks she's old enough for more privileges, a larger allowance, or a later bedtime, this is the time and place to discuss it.

4. Financial matters that involve the entire family can be discussed here, too. Has the light bill or water bill gotten out of hand? Do parents want the kids to vote on some issue such as choosing to spend money on a week's vacation at Disney World as opposed to a new swimming pool? Have you decided on across-the-board allowance raises for the kids? Here's a fine opportunity to share the good news.

5. This is also an excellent place to settle family grievances. Does Jenny feel Rob doesn't do enough household chores? Does Matt feel that Lizzie leaves stuff strewn around the family room only when it's his turn to clean in there? Air and settle, if you can, these and other problems in the context of a Family Council Meeting.

6. Make it clear which items are debatable, which ones the kids get to vote on, and which ones are simply announced. Apply basic rules of justice and parliamentary procedure. Parents obviously retain the right to overrule when needed.

Helpful Hint: Avoid thorny, potentially embarrassing issues that should be handled privately with your children.

Family Awards Night

There's lots of fun to be had on Family Awards Night. You could make an elaborate event out of it, awarding trophies or plaques, and even creating an awards ceremony. Once every month or two would be fine for most families. Select a regular time frame that suits your specific family needs, taking into account the number and frequency of certificates or trophies to be awarded.

Materials:
- The trophies, plaques, certificates, or related items that have been earned by any family member since the last Awards Night

Directions:
1. Carefully consider the types of activities and behaviors you want to reward on a special awards night. These could include awards for Games Night (page 69), Cleaning Competitions (page 97), Family Olympics (page 95), good report cards, or other family activities.

2. Keep in mind the number and frequency of awards you plan to give out. Decide how often you think you'd like to have a Family Awards Night.

3. Decide whether you'd like to combine Family Awards Night with any other event, such as a Family Council Meeting (page 65), or whether you'd like it to be a stand-alone event.

4. Announce to the family your intention to hold Family Awards Night regularly. Explain that all awards won or earned during the time period since the last Awards Night will be conferred at the event.

5. Decide if you want a ceremony or other hoopla to go with distributing the awards, or whether you want to keep it low-key.

Helpful Hint: Family Awards Night can also be a time to give out allowances and other rewards the kids have earned for working around the house.

Top Ten Lists

Once or twice a year, you and your kids can make up Top Ten Lists. However, unlike David Letterman's lists, these are not intended to be comedic.

Materials:
• Paper, pen, or pencil for each participant

Directions:
1. Each family member is asked to create two Top Ten lists. The first will deal with the top ten good things about the family. The other will involve the top ten things that need improvement in the family.

2. Valid complaints about any family member are permissible. Pettiness is not. Make sure your kids understand the difference.

3. All family members must keep an open mind—including the parents. If Steve writes that the number one thing needing improvement is the "overstrict rules," parents need to take the observation seriously. Parents should honestly evaluate the family's rules. If they believe they're fair, that's fine. But they should honestly assess the complaint. Maybe they really are too heavy-handed on some things. For example, they might decide the strict rules for bedtime, homework, courtesy, and eating are called for, but they might also see the need to lighten up in other areas.

4. Remember, you want the kids to be open-minded, too. You want them to take your suggestions for improvement seriously. Perhaps a good way to facilitate improvement in your kids' behavior is to demonstrate a willingness to negotiate with them and change your own.

Helpful Hint: Don't forget to emphasize the good things as well as the areas that need improvement. Give your kids a chance to discover why you're not the worst parents in the world!

Home Movies Night

You probably own a video camera and record lots of fun videos. You might even own some old 8-millimeter movies that your parents or grandparents shot years ago. But when was the last time you actually watched these home movies?

Pick a night when no one is likely to have any conflicts—band practice, a business meeting, or homework that can't be ignored. Tell the kids not to make any dates with friends for that night.

Materials:
- VCR
- All the movies you've shot with your video camera
- 8-millimeter projector, screen, and 8-millimeter movies from previous generations (optional)
- Popcorn or other suitable movie snacks

Directions:
1. Go through your collection of videotapes and/or 8-millimeter movies. Select a variety of ones that are likely to be of general interest.

2. If you're planning to screen 8-millimeter movies, make sure your projector is working, the bulb is OK, and you have a screen. (A white sheet can serve effectively).

3. Tell the kids not to make dates with friends for that night.

4. You might also want to do this as an impromptu activity one evening, deciding on the spur of the moment to watch old home movies.

5. Pop a batch of popcorn, make some Chex mix or candy apples, or provide other suitable snacks.

6. If you're planning to screen old home movies from previous generations and you have other relatives living nearby, consider inviting them to join you for the evening.

Helpful Hint: If you have old 8-millimeter home movies but no longer have a projector, consider getting the film transferred onto videotape. Many photo and video shops can do this for a reasonable price.

Family Games Night

"Mom, play something with me!" "Dad, why don't you ever play Monopoly with us?" "Joey, how come you'll play Hearts with your friends, but you won't play with me?"

Instead of complaining about not playing games together, designate one day a month as Family Games Night. The games can be boxed games, card games, or such games as Charades. You might all play the same game together, or perhaps Dad and Ginny will play chess together while Mom, Grandma, Jeff, and Tommy play Categories. Whatever the case, you'll all be together in the family room, living room, or den. You can even designate a certain group of games for Family Games Night. Keep these games stored away in a closet, to be taken out as a special treat on Games Night.

Materials:
- Boxed games, cards, dominoes, chess, checkers, and so on
- Additional materials needed to play other games you choose

Directions:
1. Decide whether this will be a regular activity or one to be enjoyed once a week or month (or only when the mood strikes).
2. Decide whether to put aside a special group of games for use only on Family Games Night and, if so, which ones.
3. Decide whether you will combine any other special treats with Games Night. For example, Games Night might also be Hot Dog Night or Casual Dining Night. Will it be a pajama party? If you don't make popcorn very often, you might do so on Games Night. Consider cooking hot dogs in the fireplace, or eating in the backyard in good weather. Allow the kids to stay up a little later than their usual bedtime.
4. If you have other relatives living nearby who also have kids, decide if you will occasionally invite them over on Games Night.

Helpful Hint: During the summer, designate one day as Family Game Day. Take a bunch of outdoor games and equipment to the local park and have fun. If you want, let your kids invite their friends to join you.

Take Me Out to the Ballgame

Even if your city isn't the proud host of a major-league baseball or NFL football team, you likely have some professional or college sports team within driving distance. Whether it's a farm-system baseball game, a minor-league hockey game, or college basketball, get out there as a family and cheer for the home team!

Materials:
- Tickets for all family members to see a ballgame
- Transportation to the game

Directions:
1. Determine what teams play in your area and, if you have more than one option, vote to determine which sport is of greatest general interest.

2. Get the team's schedule and pick a game that's of particular interest (a particularly strong opponent, perhaps) on a date that presents no conflicts.

3. If anyone in the family is unfamiliar with the sport, give them a quick lesson in how the game is played so they can better understand and enjoy what they're going to see.

4. Decide whether you want to dress in your team's colors.

5. Get tickets and go.

Helpful Hint: If your kids have several different interests, accommodate each of them by taking turns going to various sporting events.

Family Potluck Dinner

If you don't have other branches of the family living nearby, you can skip to the next item. But if you do have other family members living near you, here's a way to get together on a semiregular basis that's relatively low-maintenance and inexpensive for the host family: Have potluck or covered-dish suppers. This is a great way to encourage your family to enjoy their relatives.

Materials:
- Food
- Games

Directions:
1. Decide on a date and time.
2. Call all the nearby relatives and invite them. Coordinate their food contributions so you get a balanced menu.
3. Have games on hand for the kids to play.
4. Enjoy.

Helpful Hint: When the kids from all the family branches are old enough, it might be fun to have them cook the potluck food (with a little parental help if needed).

The Family Walk

You don't have to have a star on Hollywood's Walk of Fame to be memorialized in concrete. Your footprint or handprint can proclaim your uniqueness in any location—your family's porch, garden, or front yard. How many kids from other families can claim their parents have immortalized them in this way? It's just one more example of how belonging to your family is special!

Materials:

- 10- or 25-pound sack of instant-mix concrete (the size depends on how many steppingstones you're going to make.)
- Trowel
- Oil (either motor oil or cooking oil)
- Water
- A form for your steppingstone (What you use will depend on what's available and on what size stones you're planning to make. Possibilities include an ordinary plastic dishpan twelve to eighteen inches in diameter, the bottom of a five-gallon bucket, or a disposable aluminum cake pan.)
- A pencil, twig, or screwdriver if you plan to write in the concrete

Directions:

1. Oil the inside of the form so the concrete will easily pop out after it's dry. Following the package instructions, mix an appropriate amount of concrete.

2. Pour the concrete into the form to a depth of about two inches. Still following package instructions, stir the mix to remove the air bubbles.

3. Smooth the top surface with a trowel, concrete finishing tool, or straightedge made from a piece of lath or lumber.

4. When the concrete is partially hardened, each family member can press a footprint or handprint into it, write his or her name, draw a design, or all of the above. If you're going to inscribe words or pictures into the stone, the concrete must be sufficiently set so that the lines remain visible; if it's too liquid, the marks will disappear or blur.

5. If you're pressing your handprint into the concrete, it's best to oil your hand first; less of the semiwet concrete will stick to your hand. Wash up promptly afterward. It's easier to get concrete off when it's wet, and the stuff is slightly caustic and can irritate skin.

6. Once the concrete is dry, remove the form and place the step on the porch, along your walkway, or in the backyard.

Helpful Hint: The next time your family builds a new porch or sidewalk, let the kids make handprints and write their names and the date in the wet concrete. Years from now, all of you will appreciate this little piece of immortality.

Family Flower Garden

An advertising slogan for the florist industry suggests that you "Say It with Flowers." Why not show your family pride and creativity by doing the same? Plant a flower bed that proclaims your family's name or Motto (page 26) in a rich mass of colorful and fragrant blossoms!

Materials:
• Flower seeds or bedding plants
• Gardening tools (shovels, rakes, trowels, gloves, watering cans, and so on)

Directions:
1. If you've chosen family colors, decide whether they lend themselves to a garden. If so, decide what flowers (or plants) you will need in order to produce these colors. Consider climate conditions and restrictions.

2. Decide whether you want to spell out the family name, your individual first names, the Family Motto, or some combination of these.

3. Decide where you will plant the flowers or plants. Consider the front yard, where the world can see the results of your family pride at work. A shade tree out front might prevent this, so choose the next best place. How about a spot that's visible from the family room window?

4. Prepare the soil in the flower bed for the planting of your seeds or plants.

5. Plant according to the instructions on the seed packets, or according to any instructions the plant nursery gives you.

6. Tend the flower bed. Weed, prune, water, fertilize, and do whatever else is necessary to help the flowers grow.

Helpful Hint: The younger kids will enjoy digging in the dirt. Tell family stories and sing songs while tilling the soil and planting the seeds.

Family Flower Poster

If you enjoy planting and maintaining a Family Flower Garden (page 74) during the spring and summer, you're going to miss it during the cold season. But don't despair—you can keep the spirit of your family flower garden alive during the cold months with a Family Flower Poster!

Materials:
- A large piece of brown wrapping paper (the exact size will depend largely on the length of your family's last name or Motto (page 26), and the amount of wall space available.)
- Pictures of flowers cut from seed catalogues, old magazines, or other sources
- Scissors
- Glue

Directions:
1. Carefully cut pictures of individual flowers from magazines, seed catalogues, or other colorful sources. Cut around each flower to eliminate the background. Try to find flower pictures that are reasonably close to each other in size.
2. "Plant" the flowers by arranging them on the brown paper so that they spell out your family name, Motto, or both . . . or anything else appropriate to family pride.
3. When you're pleased with the arrangement, glue the flowers onto the brown paper.
4. You can create a frame or border for the brown paper by gluing more flower pictures along the four edges.
5. Hang the finished product in your family room, hallway, or other suitable location.

Helpful Hint: Make sure younger kids are carefully supervised while handling scissors.

Family Vacation: Research

Got a vacation coming up and no definite plans? Then involve the whole family in researching the possibilities. The kids will be even more excited anticipating what their research has produced, and vacation will have a special meaning when it finally arrives.

Materials:
• Travel brochures
• Access to a local library and/or the Internet
• Telephone, newspapers, or magazines

Directions:
1. First, establish your limitations and requirements. Decide if you want to restrict yourself with any of the following:
   • Places within easy driving distance
   • Places you can drive to without an overnight stay
   • Places you can fly to in the United States
   • Places in your home state
   • Vacations that cost less than a certain amount
   • Hotels that accept pets
   • Places where there's a campground
   • Places that have RV facilities or wheelchair accessibility

2. Have all family members ask their friends, classmates, coworkers, and neighbors for vacation suggestions based on their experiences.

3. Research the Internet. If you don't have a computer and modem, you can probably find one connected to the Internet at a local library.

4. Visit a travel agent and get brochures for interesting destinations.

5. Read newspaper and magazine ads for vacation destinations. When you see ones that look exciting, write to the addresses or call the toll-free numbers to request brochures and other information.

6. After everyone has gathered sufficient information, hold a Family Council Meeting (page 65) to discuss the possibilities you've discovered.

Helpful Hint: Parents should decide whether to hold a family vote or make the decision themselves. Everyone should be encouraged to present their findings and lobby for a particular destination.

Family Vacation: Countdown Calendar

Anticipation can be great fun! When you're planning a family vacation, the days and weeks leading up to your actual departure can be filled with excitement as you prepare for the adventure. Whether you're heading to your usual campsite, visiting your favorite cousins across the country, or going to a theme park, looking forward can be nearly as much fun as the actual visit. So make a Countdown Calendar to get the whole family excited and ready for the trip.

Materials:
• Commercial or homemade calendar (not one you use normally)
• Fine-line markers

Directions:

1. Get a free calendar or make one yourself (page 43) at least two months, if possible, before your vacation starts. Ask at your bank, gas station, insurance agency, or veterinarian's office about gift calendars left over from the first of the year.

2. Using a fine-line marker, preferably colored, mark a big V on each of the calendar days that the family will be on vacation. If you intend to drive several days to your destination, start the Vs on the day you will leave home, not the day you will arrive.

3. On the calendar square designating the date before your vacation is to start, write the number 1. On the square for the date before that, write the number 2. On the square before that, write the number 3, and so on. Continue until you reach the current date's square.

4. Any preparations that need to be made for the trip should be written on the calendar.

5. Each night, draw a line through that date's square.

6. Anyone who wants to know "How much longer till we go to the lake?" or "How many more days till we go see Grandma?" can find the answer for himself by looking at the calendar.

Helpful Hint: Encourage the kids to draw pictures on the calendar imagining what the vacation destination will look like.

Family Vacation: Journal/Scrapbook

Even if you're already keeping a Family Journal (page 6) or Family Scrapbook (page 7), why not keep a special journal and scrapbook for each family vacation?

Materials:
- Blank scrapbook, pen, tape or glue
- Items such as ticket stubs, vacation brochures, event programs, postcards, and other suitable memorabilia

Directions:
1. Decide how you will record journal entries every evening. You might choose one of the following options:
   - One person is chosen as the official recorder. This person writes in the journal after hearing stories from all family members.
   - Each member takes a daily turn as the official recorder.
   - Each member writes in the journal every night. Kids who are not old enough to write can dictate to a parent or an older sibling. Years from now, you'll appreciate each handwritten entry. However, find ways to avoid duplication with this strategy.
2. Be diligent about recording the day's events. Evening is usually a good time to reflect on the day's happenings before the rich details begin to fade.
3. If you have an evening activity that runs late, start the next morning by recording events from the day before.
4. Leave room to glue or tape postcards, programs, and other memorabilia onto pages of the journal/scrapbook. It might be a good idea to put the memorabilia in a folder at the back of the book. You can glue them in their proper places when you get home. You might want to paper-clip the memento on the relevant journal page until you get home. That way you'll know where everything should go.

Helpful Hint: If you're always too tired at the end of the day, or you don't want to take the time to write journal entries during the vacation, you might consider recording the stories on audiotapes and writing them down when you get home.

Family Vacation: Our Special Place

Does your family have a special memory of a vacation that everyone loved? Was it affordable? Most families get to visit Disney World only once or twice in a lifetime, but trips to the cabin or campground are usually within financial reach. If you find someplace you love that agrees with the budget, consider returning there on a regular basis. This one special place can fill your family with enough good memories to last a lifetime.

Materials: None

Directions:

1. If you've found one special place where the whole family enjoys vacationing, discuss the possibility of making it your special family vacation spot.

2. Discuss the fact that this probably means you won't explore other vacation possibilities as much. Usually vacation time is limited, and if you like going to the beach house, you might not have time to go anywhere else. Make sure this is satisfactory to everyone.

3. Discuss affordability. Can the family budget permit an annual vacation at the cabin resort up north and a trip out of state? You might discover that both parents and kids are willing to reduce everyday expenses for movies, eating out, and so on in exchange for being able to return to the beach house. Both the sacrifices made and the commitment to a special family vacation will strengthen your family's bonds and increase family pride.

4. If the family agrees and the prospect seems affordable, select your particular location as Our Special Place. Remember, you can always change your mind in two or three years if your interests change.

Helpful Hint: Try to find a special vacation spot that still allows you to take at least one other vacation trip per year. Traditions are great, but variety is the spice of life!

Family Dictionary

The special words and expressions coined by your family members and the meanings associated with known words are all part of what makes your family unique.

Maybe you refer to "dust bunnies" as "fuzz stuff." Or maybe you call the coins and crud that accumulate under sofa cushions "pocket dirt." Compile these words and phrases in your family dictionary!

Materials:
- Paper, hole fasteners, pen (or computer or typewriter)
- Construction paper
- Crayons or fine-line markers

Directions:
1. At a Family Council Meeting (page 65) or informal gathering, make a list of special family words and their meanings. These can be either totally made-up words (or phrases) or real words that have a special meaning or usage within your family.

2. Write each word or phrase and its definition on paper. You can put each word on a separate sheet, if you like. If anyone can remember the origin of a word or phrase—how it came to be used by your family—write that down, too.

3. You might want to include illustrations.

4. If you've included only one word on a page, arrange the pages in alphabetical order.

5. Create a construction-paper cover for your dictionary. You'll probably want to include a title on your finished book, such as *The Johnson Family Dictionary*. Make sure to include a list of all the family members. You might also include a credits page listing the names of family members who compiled and edited the manuscript. You could also illustrate the cover with a picture or design, and construct a back cover out of construction paper as well.

6. Assemble the covers and contents and bind the book with hole fasteners. As new words and phrases enter your family's lexicon, add them to the dictionary.

Helpful Hint: You might want to include pronunciation instructions after each word, the way a regular dictionary would.

Family Bedtime Stories

Your kids' favorite stories may be *Rapunzel* or *Sleeping Beauty,* but I bet they'd enjoy hearing about your first car, your first bike, your wedding day, or the funny story about Grandma and the chickens! What better time to tell them your own stories than at night when the kids are cozy in bed and ready for a good tale? You can teach them family history and instill pride in their family while you're getting them ready for sleep.

Materials:
• Memories of family events

Directions:
1. Get the kids ready for their bedtime story. Instead of reading from *Jack and the Beanstalk* or *Aladdin,* tell them family stories about any of the following and more:

 • The night they were born
 • The house you grew up in, and how it compares with your present house
 • Collecting eggs when you spent the summer on Uncle Henry's farm
 • How Great-Great-Grandpa came over from Ireland, or Ethiopia, or England, or Istanbul, or wherever

Helpful Hint: You might want to alternate family stories with other book stories, depending on what your kids want to hear.

Cumulative Bedtime Stories

This is a fun activity that can involve the whole family. Like Writing Bedtime Stories (page 84), your kids will have an opportunity to stretch their creative muscles, with a little help, of course.

Materials: A good imagination

Directions:

1. One person starts. It might be easiest to have a parent start the first time, until the kids get the hang of it. Once your kids are familiar with the activity, they will clamor for the opportunity to begin a story.

2. Start telling a story. It can be about anyone or anything, but should involve a bit of adventure and excitement. After someone narrates for a few minutes, stop the story and let the next person take over. This works best if you stop at some crucial juncture in the story— like when Jamie finds the suitcase in the middle of the sidewalk, or when Pat sees the spaceship land, or when the wolf is chasing the brave little chicken.

3. The next person picks up where the previous person left off, but don't be surprised if the story takes a sudden turn and the action moves from Ginny's backyard to a secret tunnel under the mysterious professor's old mansion. Encourage the narrator to break off telling the story at an exciting point in the action.

4. Continue taking turns until everyone has had a chance. If only two people are involved, take turns back and forth until it's time to go to sleep.

5. Continue in this way until someone ends the story, or until it seems to be losing energy and interest.

6. If it's still too early for lights-out, you can always start another story. On the other hand, if your kids tend to get really caught up in this activity, you might need to start story time earlier in the evening!

Helpful Hint: Group storytelling might be easier in the family room after everyone has cleaned up and put on pajamas. If you have only one child, then you could tell stories in bed. (You could also do this if several kids share a bedroom.)

Bedtime Stories:
Your Kid's Turn to Read

Anyone can read bedtime stories to their kids. Why not do things differently and reverse the roles—let the kids read to you! Your kids will enjoy acting like grown-ups, and they'll enjoy demonstrating their reading ability. This activity might also encourage them to become even better readers so they can display their reading skills to you.

For younger kids not reading yet, let them *tell* you a familiar story or a made-up story.

Materials:
• A book

Directions:
1. Curl up together on your child's bed. If many kids are involved and they don't share a bedroom, you could recline on the sofa together.

2. Let your child select the night's story and then read that story aloud to you. If there are two or more kids in your family who have already learned to read, let them take turns on different nights or have them each read a story to you.

3. Have younger kids not reading yet tell a familiar story aloud, usually something they've heard a million times. Your child probably knows *Cinderella* or *The Three Little Pigs* by heart. Don't worry if she can't tell the story exactly as it happened—let her exercise creative freedom.

4. Tell her how well she's done, kiss her good night, and bask in the knowledge that you're raising a family of readers!

Helpful Hint: With more than one reader, it might be fun to have everyone listen while one person reads a story. But if your kids get restless, have them read quietly until their turn comes.

Write Bedtime Stories

Kids certainly need consistency and structure, but occasionally it's fun to vary the nightly routine. A little change can provide a special treat for everyone. Also, kids are natural storytellers, and it's important to stimulate their creativity. Mix these factors together and you have the recipe for a great bedtime activity: Make up original bedtime stories! Most kids have heard or can read a Robin Hood story, but how many of them enjoy the legend of the "storytelling daisy" before going to bed?

Materials:
• A good imagination

Directions:
1. Instead of reading one of the usual books, make up a story all your own and tell it to your child(ren) at night.

2. Encourage your kids whenever they're interested to provide a nightly story themselves. Have them take turns telling a story they've invented.

3. Sometimes their "original" stories will sound more like a collage of other favorite stories. Be patient. They're learning to stretch their imaginations. In time, their minds will soar and their stories will sound less and less like what they've heard.

4. Be patient but firm if the kids are clamoring to take a turn. If it's Jason's turn tonight, it can be Lisa's turn tomorrow. If Jason's story is short, perhaps there'll be time for both to tell a story before lights-out.

5. Encourage your kids but don't force them. If they're initially reluctant, try making a suggestion:
   • What do you think happened to the Seven Dwarfs after Snow White went off to marry her prince?
   • Did Cinderella and Prince Charming have kids? Why don't you tell me about them?
   • Tell me a story about a boy who took a ride on a cloud.
   • Tell me about a girl who built a ladder to climb to the sky and catch a star to wish on.

Helpful Hint: Don't insist that your kids tell a story. One child might enjoy it, but another might not. Let them decide.

Create a Picture Book of Your Own Story

Kids are natural storytellers (see Write Bedtime Stories, page 84), and they love to be the center of attention—both as the author and the subject of a story. They also love picture books. What do you get when you put these things together? You wind up with your child writing a story by himself, about himself, and turning it into a picture book!

Materials:
- White construction paper or typing paper
- Fine-line colored markers or crayons
- Typewriter or computer or pen
- Two sheets of light-colored construction paper
- Stapler

Directions:
1. Encourage your child to write a story about herself. She can write it in pen or use a typewriter or computer, if you have one. Be sure she writes on only one side of the paper (white typing paper or construction paper). The story can be either fiction or nonfiction.

2. Let your child draw a front and back cover for her book, using light-colored construction paper for the covers. On the front cover, be sure to include the title ("My Visit to the Mountains"), the byline ("by Jennifer Schwartz"), and illustrations. The back cover will probably include another illustration.

3. Be sure the pages are in order, then staple the book together.

4. On the back of each page (except for the inside of the front cover), have your child draw a picture that illustrates the opposite page.

5. Let your child read her story to you.

Helpful Hint: A third-grader can probably spell well enough to handle this activity on his own. A younger child will need lots of help. A child who can't write yet can still dictate the book to a parent or older sibling, though that might not be as much fun.

Family Newscast

Most kids are natural hams. Wouldn't it be fun to have them report the day's news like Peter Jennings? They'll get to practice their writing and public-speaking skills, and everyone will stay informed on the daily happenings in family life.

Materials:
- Paper
- Pen or pencil or computer or typewriter

Directions:
1. Have each child report his own news (events he witnessed by himself).
2. Tell your kids to write a news summary about each event of the day that they deem newsworthy. These might include items about school, other family members, pets, and general human interest stories. Did Tommy next-door break his arm? Did the Wilsons' dog get out and run loose all over the neighborhood?
3. Give the kids ten minutes or more of prep time, depending on how much news there is. "Broadcast" time might range from two to twenty minutes, depending on volume and depth of coverage.
4. Have the kids take turns daily being the news anchor. If you have more than one child, the other siblings will act as "on the scene" reporters. The anchor greets the audience and reports the lead story, then calls upon another reporter for a follow-up or a different story. In a family with only one child—or only one old enough to take part in this activity—the anchor will have to carry the newscast singlehandedly.
5. Don't allow the newscast to degenerate into a tattletale session, with the activity an excuse for the kids to report on each other's transgressions.
6. When the anchor and reporters have read all their news stories for the night, the anchor should remember to sign off, including a reminder to his audience to be sure and tune in tomorrow.

Helpful Hint: Parents should help kids decide how to handle stories involving more than one family member.

Family Band

You don't need major talent to play in a family band. It's a fun activity that brings the family together.

Materials:

• Instruments (real or improvised ones, such as a comb or water glass)

Directions:

1. Have each family member choose an instrument. These might include a triangle, harmonica, water glasses filled to different levels, and so on. With older kids, you might include more serious instruments such as a piano, violin, saxophone, or drums.

2. Make music together. If you'll pardon my co-opting a famous old saying, "The family that plays together stays together."

Helpful Hint: Consider arranging a time for family rehearsals. You could even schedule an occasional concert for the extended family.

Family Rhythm Band

The whole family can get together on this one and prove they're "in tune" in more ways than one—even if no one can play even the kazoo. All it takes is a recording of regular music and a few home-made percussion "instruments" for the family to play along.

Materials:
- Music recording (tape, CD, even LP!) and player
- Instruments, either store-bought or homemade (these could include a pot and a wooden spoon to beat against a surface, two wooden spoons to beat together, a ring binder or book to beat your hand on, a triangle, cymbals, drums, and so on.)

Directions:
1. Turn on the music.
2. Beat your instrument in time to the rhythm.
3. Have fun!

Helpful Hint: You might want to do this with doors and windows closed, or down in the basement.

Open Mike Night

What about the family that has talents other than playing music? Have an Open Mike Night! If Dad is a computer doofus who doesn't know a mouse from an icon, or Mom is hopelessly mired in "old" music, the kids may legitimately wonder about you. Maybe it's time to reveal your hidden talents!

Open Mike Night is a great opportunity for coaxing shy kids out of their shells, for showing them their undiscovered talents, and for proving to your kids you know how to do something other than driving carpools and yelling about messy rooms.

If you have a child who is reluctant to perform, have her start out as the M.C. Being a good M.C. is an important talent, too!

Materials:
- Whatever your particular talents or skills require, such as tap shoes, a copy of the story you wrote, props for magic tricks, and so on

Directions:
1. Have everyone decide what to perform. Options might include the following:
   - Telling jokes
   - Playing an instrument
   - Singing a song
   - Reciting poetry
   - Giving a dramatic reading or monologue
   - Staging a dance or acrobatics exhibition
   - Displaying and discussing artwork
   - Reading a story you've written

2. Choose one family member to be the M.C. Have her announce all the acts. If everyone in the family wants to participate as a performer, one family member can perform and also double as M.C.

3. Have each family member take turns performing. They can perform more than once, if you like, either by singing one song early in the show and another later, or by telling jokes now and doing magic later.

Helpful Hint: Your kids might want to collaborate on certain acts. That's fine. This might be a good way to help the shy ones.

Family Chorus

If "the family that prays together stays together," then "the family that sings together . . . does fun things together!" Though any kind of group singing is fun, harmony and counterpoint and rounds make this a true family activity.

Materials:
- Recorded music to give you the melody and words you need (if necessary)

Directions:
1. To sing counterpoint, find two songs that can be sung simultaneously and also work well opposite each other. An example might be "Pine Cones and Hollyberries" and "It's Beginning to Look a Lot Like Christmas." In fact, this combination can be found on a number of Christmas music albums. Equal numbers of family members sing each song.
2. Rounds are songs like "Row, Row, Row Your Boat," in which different people can come into the song at different points, each starting a little later on. "Row, Row, Row Your Boat" can be sung as a two-part round with the second group coming in on "Merrily, Merrily," or as a four-part round with groups coming in on "Gently," "Merrily," and "Life."
3. In harmony, both halves of the group usually sing the same words, but their tune is different. There are various kinds of harmony, the most notable being the barbershop quartet. Consult a harmony book for detailed instructions.

Helpful Hint: It might be fun to have younger voices sing opposite older ones in rounds.

Book of Family Songs

Does your family love to sing together? Do you sing in the car, while you pull weeds in the yard, or while you wash dishes? You probably have some favorite songs, and there are probably others the family knows but doesn't always think about singing. Why not compile a book of your family's favorite songs?

Materials:
- Paper
- Pen or typewriter or computer
- Stapler

Directions:
1. Get together and make a list of all the songs the family likes to sing together.
2. Have one person—probably a parent or older child—write down all the words to every song. You can also allow different family members to write down the words to different songs.
3. Get together and make sure you agree on the way the words have been written down. Most of us know about the kids who think the words to "God Bless America" include "through the night with the light from a bulb."
4. If you like, you can make copies of the words, either by photocopying or printing extra copies from your computer. That way every family member can have a copy.
5. Staple your songbook(s) together.
6. Sing!

Helpful Hint: You might want to consult a book of lyrics for accurate information if members can't agree on what's correct.

Family Theater

Your family can have fun putting on shows for friends and neighbors, or for no audience at all. Family Theater is an enterprise that brings the family together and will certainly spark feelings of pride within each member of your family's theatrical troupe!

Materials:
- Props as required by the show being performed
- Individual copies of a script written by one or more members of the family (optional)

Directions:
1. Get together and agree on what show you're going to perform. It will probably be a favorite story such as *Aladdin* or *The Three Little Pigs*. It could also be a family story such as the unusual story of how Grandma and Grandpa met, or some other family adventure that takes more than five or ten minutes to enact. You can even write an original play that's not based on any previous story.

2. Agree on whether you're going to write a script or ad-lib the action.

3. If you're scripting it, then first write the script. You can collaborate or leave it for one family member who's particularly talented at writing.

4. Assign a part to every family member unless someone prefers to be the audience. Have everyone learn his part—whether it's scripted or ad-libbed.

5. Assemble any props and scenery you need.

6. Rehearse.

7. Put on the performance. You can act for the sheer fun of it, or you can assemble a larger audience of friends and family. If the show is a family story, put it on when the cousins come to visit. If it's a famous old favorite, put it on for the neighbors or visiting friends.

Helpful Hint: Make sure to help the younger ones learn their roles and lines.

Family Puppet Theater

This activity is similar to Family Theater (page 92) except that instead of live actors, you're using puppets. Again, you can enact a traditional favorite story, a family story, or an original story.

Materials:
- Props as required by the show being performed
- Puppets—homemade or store-bought (For sock puppets you will need one white or pale sock, three or more buttons, a fine-line marker, yarn, glue, scissors, and a rubber band for each puppet.)
- Card table lying on its side or a table with a sheet or tablecloth draped over the front, to hide the puppeteers
- Individual copies of a script (optional)

Directions:
1. Get together and agree on what show you're going to perform.
2. Agree on whether you're going to write a script or ad-lib the action.
3. If you're scripting it, then write the script. You can collaborate or "hire" one family member who's particularly talented at writing.
4. Decide whether you're going to use store-bought puppets (you may have some at home already) or homemade ones.
5. If making sock puppets (they're probably easiest), stuff cotton into the farthest half of a sock (from the toes to the heel) to create the head. Wrap a rubber band below that to create a neck and keep the cotton in place. Sew two buttons in place for the eyes, one button for the nose, and either a row of buttons or a line drawn for the mouth. Glue yarn on top of the head for hair. Cut two holes in the sock where the arms would go, not far below the rubber band. Stick a finger through each hole for the puppet's "arms."
6. Assign a part to every family member who wants to participate. Have everyone learn her part—whether it's scripted or ad-libbed.
7. Assemble any props and scenery you need and rehearse.
8. Put on the performance.

Helpful Hint: Help the younger kids learn their lines.

Pet Show

Your family can organize a pet show involving all your friends or everyone on your block. You'll have fun showing off your family pet or pets, and you can enjoy the pride of knowing you organized the whole event yourself.

Materials:
- The family pet(s)
- Flyers publicizing the event throughout the neighborhood (optional)
- Blue construction paper, scissors, and a black fine-line marker (for making blue "ribbons" with "Winner" written on them)

Directions:
1. Decide when and where you're going to have the pet show, and whether or not you're going to give prizes. If you intend to give prizes, select the categories (best pet, best dog, best cat, cutest pet, ugliest pet, and so on).

2. Decide who the judges will be.

3. Let your neighbors and friends know that you're putting on a pet show. If you like, put up flyers on local phone poles or leave them in neighbors' front doors.

4. On the day of the pet show, have each child or family display a pet or pets.

5. Award prizes, if you've decided to do so.

Helpful Hint: You might want to include family *and* friends, to increase the number of pets in the show.

Family Olympics

One way to nourish family pride and spirit is to compete in athletic events against other families. In the real Olympics, Americans compete with the British, Australians, Germans, Japanese, and so on. Your family can compete with the Turners, O'Briens, Lees, and Shapiros.

Many Americans do not consider themselves stridently patriotic, but when the Olympics come around, they suddenly find themselves rooting boisterously for American athletes. Imagine this same transformation in your family.

Materials:
- Whatever events you choose to have in your Olympics
- Paper and pen for creating certificates to reward the winner of each event (optional)

Directions:
1. Decide on a location that's suitable. Your backyard is fine if it's large enough, especially if you have a basketball net or other sports equipment. A public park or city playground might be better.

2. Contact other families, preferably ones whose kids are about the same age as yours. Agree on a date that works for all participants (and an alternate date in case it rains). If you're planning several events, you may want to spread the Olympics out over a weekend.

3. Families should gather to select a set of events in which everyone will compete. Use the real Olympics as a model. Events might include relay races, basketball competitions, croquet, horseshoes, quoits, jacks, jump rope, apple bobbing, balloon races, and so on. You can also include such events as cooking and baking. You can even have a contest to see which family can pick up the most litter from the streets of your town in two hours.

4. If you want to, design an award certificate for the winner of each event.

5. Hold your Olympics. If you have decided to award certificates to the winners, fill in the appropriate individual or team name on the applicable certificate as each event concludes.

Helpful Hint: Find events that allow even the youngest kids to participate actively.

Card or Game Tournament

Who's the family champ at gin rummy? Do you have a dominoes champion, Monopoly expert, or word-game champion?

It would be fun to host a family game night or an elimination tournament over a series of days. You could include all members of the household or hold competitions strictly among the kids. You could have a Scrabble tournament one weekend and a Parcheesi competition the next. Also, you could award a point to the winner of each family game, and declare the member who winds up with the most points the grand champion! However you work it out, it's bound to be a lot of fun!

Materials:
- Whatever equipment is required for the game(s) you're playing
- Homemade or store-bought plaques, trophies, or ribbons to present to the winners

Directions:
1. Work out the details:
    - Decide how you want to structure the competition. Will you have only Hearts or Payday, or will you play five or ten different games, awarding points to each winner and declaring the person who wins the most points the grand champion?
    - Decide how many times you will play the game before declaring a champion.
    - Decide whether you want single- or double-elimination competitions, where losers are either immediately eliminated or moved to more difficult brackets.
2. Decide how you will award prizes. It might be fun to have both individual and overall champions.
3. Decide what your prizes will be: trophies, ribbons, plaques, or novel awards such as ice-cream treats or being excused from chores for one week.
4. Hold an awards ceremony if you like.

Helpful Hint: Try to find games that will allow every kid to win at least once. Remember, the underlying goal is family pride and unity. Everybody needs to feel good at something.

Cleaning Competition

Turn housecleaning into a competition, and you may get the kids so eager to outdo each other that they complete all their chores without a single complaint!

Materials:
- Housecleaning supplies
- A trophy or novel award

Directions:

1. Decide which chores the kids will do, such as mopping, vacuuming, changing the sheets, doing the laundry, dusting, and so on.

2. Decide whether you'll award a trophy or novel item to the winner of the week (or month), or whether you'll award temporary possession of a general's cap to the current leader. The wearer gets to do a certain amount of bossing-around, as generals are inclined to do. This may appeal to kids more than a trophy. But remember: It's all in good fun, and the bottom line is family pride.

3. Decide who will judge the kids' efforts.

4. Decide the method of judging:
   - Each child's performance receives one to ten points, depending on how well the job was done. (Age should be taken into consideration, of course.) At the end of a month, the child who has racked up the most points is declared champion of the month.
   - You might want to choose a weekly champ as well, using the same point system.
   - Kids alternate chores from week to week, so that each child has a chance to be judged at dusting, mopping, and so on. At the end of a cycle, when each child has done each chore once, a winner is declared and a new cycle is started.

5. Ownership of the trophy or plaque—if you use that system—is temporary. When a new champion is declared, the old champ passes the trophy to the new winner.

Helpful Hint: Make sure the evaluation system is clearly understood and approved by everyone before competition begins. The kids should know exactly how they can receive a high score.

Family Trophy

Kids are naturally competitive. In most families, this leads to perennial squabbles. One approach to managing this competitiveness is to channel it: Instead of having to deal with the kids fighting over petty stuff, redirect their energies so that they're competing in a healthier way.

You can find healthy competitions elsewhere in this book, such as the Cleaning Competition (page 97) and Card or Game Tournament (page 96). There are many positive ways for the kids to compete. Also, you can offer a trophy or certificate to be rotated periodically throughout the family.

Materials:
• Trophy, certificate, or novel award

Directions:
1. Decide what events you're going to award trophies for and how often. This could be a daily occurrence, such as giving a prize for good manners. It could also be a weekly or seasonal event, such as awarding a trophy to every kid who rakes a big pile of leaves in ten minutes.

2. Announce what the award will be.

3. Buy or make the trophy or certificate or other prize.

4. When the competition is over, award the prize to the winner and include a ceremony if you like. Avoid making it so corny that the kids groan.

Helpful Hint: Make sure the kids clearly understand the ground rules.

Gift-Giving Traditions

There are plenty of ways to give to charity besides dropping a quarter in the kettle during the winter holidays or donating time at the local soup kitchen. Here are a few ideas for showing your kids how to give from their hearts. In so doing, they will become active members in the family's tradition of giving.

Materials:
- Money (optional)
- Toys, books, and unwanted clothes still in decent condition (optional)
- New gifts you've received but do not want (optional)

Directions:
1. Decide how you would like to give to charity. You can either gather as a family to make a group decision, or you can allow individual members to make independent decisions. Choose one or more of the ideas below, or any others you come up with:

   - Set aside a percentage of your allowance, birthday and holiday gift money, earnings from your paper route, or a portion of each of these for a favorite charity.
   - Volunteer your time regularly at a local charity to sort merchandise donations, stuff envelopes, serve food in a soup kitchen, or help transport donated items to local families in need.
   - Donate your unwanted clothes, outgrown toys and books, and other items to a local charity, hospital, daycare center, or other good cause.
   - Donate unwanted gifts to charity, like a sweater that's the wrong color or a game you already have.

Helpful Hint: Help younger kids learn how to make good charitable decisions. Some kids are so generous, they want to give everything away!

Family Kitty

Everybody loves kitties—both the ones that purr and the ones that fill up with money. While many families use the second type for the kids' college fund or family vacations, you could also contribute a portion of it to charity.

Materials:
- A piggy bank, jar, or other container

Directions:
1. Decide what charity will benefit from your family kitty.
2. Decide how often the kitty money should be sent to charity. You might select a time frame such as every six months or year, or you could wait until a certain dollar amount has been accumulated before sending.
3. Decide how family members will contribute and how much. Here are some possibilities:
   - Every time a family member breaks a rule or commits some other offense such as not washing the dishes, leaving his toys in the family room, or barging into his sister's room when the door is closed, he is fined and required to pay the piggy.
   - Every time a family member uses unacceptable language, she has to pay the piggy. Parents decide what words or phrases are unacceptable.
   - Every family member is required to pay a certain amount weekly out of his allowance or outside earnings. Establishing a percentage is a good policy, since siblings might earn different amounts depending on their responsibilities.
   - All money found in the cracks of the sofa, under chair cushions, or outside goes into the kitty.
   - If your family sells recyclable materials, those proceeds could go into the kitty.
   - Similarly, proceeds from yard sales or lemonade stands could feed the piggy.

Helpful Hint: Help kids develop an appreciation for charitable giving. These gifts should not be resented as "taxes" on allowances or other earned income.

Family Business

Most kids love to earn money. If you belong to a particularly enterprising family, you could start a family business! Whether it's a one-time undertaking or an ongoing venture, there's nothing like pulling together for a shared goal. Donate a portion to your favorite charity.

Materials: (for flyers)
- Colored paper
- Computer or colored fine-line markers
- Adhesive tape

Directions:
1. Hold a family meeting to decide what business you'd like to try. This could be a one-shot deal (like a yard sale), a periodic business (like a lemonade stand), or an ongoing business (like doing yard-work for the neighbors). Other possibilities include a used book or toy sale, Backyard Carnival (Page 102), bake sale, or homegrown vegetable sale.
2. Decide which charity will benefit from your earnings.
3. Make flyers advertising your enterprise. This will be easiest with a computer. Make it look professional. Print out the flyers on colored paper for a nice touch. If you don't have a computer, write your flyers by hand using colored markers. Make sure to mention that the money earned will go to charity.
4. Distribute your flyers:
   - On bulletin boards in local stores
   - On phone or electric poles
   - In neighbors' front doors
   - In school
5. If you're running a service business (mowing, shoveling, or babysitting), be diligent about showing up on time and doing a good job. Ask your customers to recommend you to their friends.
6. If you're conducting a one-time event like a comic-book sale, spread the word by telling all your friends. Ask them to tell other kids they know.

Helpful Hint: Young ones can participate in various ways that you consider safe and fun.

Backyard Carnival

A backyard carnival can be great fun for family, friends, and neighbors. You could charge either a single admission fee or various event fees, with all proceeds going to your favorite charity.

Materials:
- Materials for games to be played
- Inexpensive toys to be given as party favors and prizes for the winners
- Materials to make homemade flyers advertising the event

Directions:

1. Hold a family meeting and decide the following:
   - Who will be invited
   - How you plan to charge people
   - Which charity will benefit from the carnival proceeds
   - Which games and activities you want to have
   - How various games and activities will be administered
   - How you intend to advertise

2. Assemble the materials and start spreading the word.

3. Here are just a few game suggestions:
   - Trick basketball shots in your backyard hoop
   - Hula-Hoop toss (Throw a ball through a Hula-Hoop from a distance.)
   - Hungry clown (Throw a small ball or a rolled-up pair of socks through the cut-out mouth of a clown painted on a piece of wood.)
   - Bobbing for apples
   - Bop the jug (Using a ball, try to knock over a plastic milk jug partially filled with beans, barley, or sand.)
   - Pyramid can toss (Set up a pyramid of ten empty soda cans, and give each contestant three tries to knock over all ten cans.)
   - Sheet ball (Try to fit a large ball through a not-much-larger hole cut into a discarded sheet or tablecloth.)
   - Mini golf (Use a yardstick to hit a Ping-Pong ball or jacks ball into cans lying on their sides—their tops should be completely removed and any sharp edges filed down.)

Helpful Hint: Give everyone in the family a chance to design and administer the games.

Neighborhood Auction

A neighborhood auction is a wonderful way to sell homemade crafts and get rid of gifts you don't want. It's also an opportunity to get together with your neighbors. And best of all, you can donate the money earned to charity.

Materials:
- Materials for homemade flyers advertising the auction
- Unwanted books, toys, CDs, cassettes, gifts, and other items you want to get rid of
- Homemade items you want to sell (knitted sweaters, crocheted stuffed animals, bookends, baked goods, or other handicrafts)

Directions:
1. Decide which families will participate and invite them to a meeting.

2. At the meeting, decide who will attend the auction.

3. Select a date and time. Decide which items will be eligible for sale. You might want to include categories other than those mentioned above (for example, services like baby-sitting, lawnmowing, and so on).

4. Decide which charity will benefit from the auction.

5. If you're advertising to the general public, put people in charge of posters, flyers, press releases, and so on.

6. Select one person to function as auctioneer and one person to coordinate the items presented on the auction block.

7. Decide where the auction will be held.

8. If you're inviting the general public, put someone in charge of getting any necessary permits.

9. Select or create the items your family wants to sell at the auction.

Helpful Hint: Most responsibilities should be handled by older children and adults, but younger kids can help by contributing their crafts.

Adopt a Street

You don't live only in your house. You live in a neighborhood, a city, a state, a country, and the world. But let's start small—with your immediate surroundings. Help your kids develop a strong sense of community involvement by having them take pride in their neighborhood. One way is to adopt a street—either your own or one in your immediate area.

Materials:
- Trash bags
- Rubber gloves
- Flower seeds
- Weeding implements (at least a trowel)
- Other people as needed

Directions:
1. Hold a family meeting and agree to adopt a street, preferably in your own neighborhood or one nearby.

2. Agree on what jobs will be done. You might decide to at least clean up any litter lying on the sidewalk and in the street near the curb. You might also want to plant flowers in the swail area or around trees that are set in holes in the concrete. This will depend on whether you live in the city, suburbs, or country. You may choose other beautification or maintenance tasks as required.

3. Depending on your kids' ages, decide whether family members will go out together or alone. Also agree on how often you will patrol the neighborhood. Once a week or month might work well.

4. Make sure your kids know the safety rules regarding picking up trash. Have them wear rubber gloves and avoid dangerous objects like glass. Also instruct them to avoid going out into the street to retrieve litter.

5. If needed, post a schedule of street maintenance so that nobody forgets.

6. Clean the street faithfully.

Helpful Hint: Younger kids need to be carefully supervised. Contact relevant city officials to ask them about any cleanup ordinances that should be followed.

Neighborhood Olympics

Organize a sports event for the neighborhood. Charge an entry fee and donate the proceeds to charity. Your family will be remembered as the driving force behind this charitable effort, and your kids will learn the importance of doing for others.

Materials:
- Materials for homemade flyers
- Accessories for the various events

Directions:

1. Consider what types of sporting events you could have in the competition. These could include conventional sporting events such as a 100-meter dash, bicycle race, basketball competition, and so on. You could also include unconventional events such as a Hula-Hoop contest, yo-yo competition, jacks competition, skateboard race, and so on. Select a location too. If your street isn't quiet, pick a place with no traffic.

2. Decide what charity will benefit from the proceeds.

3. Select one or more judges (preferably a panel of three).

4. Buy or make ribbons or certificates to award to the first-prize winner in each event.

5. Make up flyers advertising the Olympics. List the events, date, time, place, entry fees, charity that will receive the proceeds, and a phone number to call for more information. Make the fees affordable so kids can enter several events each.

6. If you want to use your own street, contact the city and see what permits you need.

Helpful Hint: Make sure you include events for younger kids, and have prizes for *all* the kids, even ones who don't win any events.

Stage a Performance

Kids love to perform, so have them put on a play, puppet show, or concert. You could charge admission and donate the proceeds to charity. As with the Neighborhood Olympics (page 105), your family will learn the importance of giving—time and energy as well as money.

Materials:
- Materials for homemade flyers
- Any instruments and props needed for the performance
- A suitable place to hold the performance

Directions:
1. Decide what type of performance you're going to put on.

2. Pick a suitable place to hold it.

3. Decide whether you need anyone outside your family to help stage the performance. Ask for help if necessary.

4. Write a play, select songs to sing, or make puppets—whatever you want to do.

5. Decide how much you're going to charge and what charity will benefit.

6. Make up flyers advertising the performance.

7. Gather any props, costumes, or other necessary equipment.

8. Plan a program and rehearse.

9. Put on the performance on the day you've selected.

Helpful Hint: For more information on how to put on a play, concert, or puppet show, see Family Theater (page 92), Family Band (page 87), or Family Puppet Show (page 93).

Neighborhood Block Party

Your family can join other families on your street for a grand neighborhood party. You can involve only the families within a few houses on either side, or all the families on your block—however many people works best for you. Make sure parents, kids, and any other generations that live nearby are invited.

Materials:
- Food
- Games
- A city or county permit if you're going to hold the party out in the street rather than in one or more backyards or houses

Directions:
1. Decide how many households to invite to the party. This will depend in part on where you live, how long your street is, and so on.
2. Choose a date and time. If it will be an outdoor party, you may also want to choose an alternate date in case of rain.
3. Select the specific location: one or more backyards, one or more houses, out in the street, and so on.
4. Apply for a permit from the city or county if you're holding it in the street.
5. Decide how to supply the food and drinks. It might be best to make it a covered-dish supper, with everyone contributing food and a beverage. Or you could delegate certain jobs to certain households.
6. Choose the games and activities for the party. If you're planning an outdoor event, you'll probably want games such as stickball, hopscotch, marbles, hide-and-seek, and tag. Make sure parents are invited to play, too!
7. Invite everyone you want to attend. If you're having a covered-dish supper, coordinate the contributions so you don't wind up with six households supplying potato salad and no one bringing a main course.
8. Relax and enjoy yourself at the party!

Helpful Hint: Make sure to include plenty of events for all age groups. Also, provide various types of food and beverages to satisfy various tastes.

White Elephant Exchange

You probably have lots of things in your closet that you'd love to get rid of. You also have lots of things you need. Why not set up an exchange where you could trade your "white elephants" for stuff other folks don't want. After all, your idea of a white elephant could easily be someone else's treasure—and vice-versa.

Materials:
- Gifts you've received but can't return
- Unwanted clothes or items that don't fit anymore (but are still in decent shape)
- Games, toys, and comic books your kids no longer want
- Cookware and other kitchenware that you no longer need
- Cassettes, CDs, books, videotapes, or other entertainment items you no longer want
- The picture hanging on the wall that you'd really love to get rid of
- Anything else that needs a new home
- Tables for spreading items out on

Directions:
1. Decide which families you're going to include in the exchange. You might invite everyone on your block.
2. Decide on a date, time, alternate date, and basic ground rules. In order to avoid a free-for-all with kids running around grabbing everything in sight, you might want to require that everyone trade one item for another. After the heavy trading is finished, you could place all unclaimed items on a table and give things away one kid at a time, starting with the youngest.
3. Spread the word to your neighbors.
4. Have fun!

Helpful Hint: Parents should approve all items their kids want to trade at the exchange, and all items their kids want to acquire.

Fun Family Holidays

Birthday: King or Queen for a Day

You can honor anyone who's having a birthday in your family and make his day really special. Whether it's a parent or one of the kids, treat the birthday person like a king or queen all day!

Materials:
- Construction paper
- Crayons or fine-line markers
- Scissors
- Glue
- Whatever ingredients you need for a special breakfast

Directions:
1. Start by serving the birthday person a special breakfast in bed.
2. On the breakfast tray, place a silly homemade Birthday Hat or Crown (page 111) with "Birthday Queen" or "Birthday King" written on it. Use construction paper to create the hat.
3. The birthday person is excused from all chores (except homework) on her birthday. If the person is Mom or Dad, the kids should help out with Mom's or Dad's chores all day.
4. If the person wants a glass of soda or a box of raisins, he has the right to ask someone else in the family to get it for him. He doesn't have to get up. It's his birthday and it comes only once a year.

Helpful Hint: Parents should make sure the kingly or queenly privilege is not abused.

Birthday Hat or Crown

How do you honor the birthday person in your family? There are many things you can do to recognize her special day. One way is to make a distinctive hat that the birthday person can wear while at home during the day. Since the person is King or Queen for the day, make the hat in the shape of a crown!

Materials:
- Yellow construction paper
- Crayon or fine-line marker
- Scissors
- Glue

Directions:
1. Make a crown out of construction paper. Cut out a long, rectangular strip of paper with little triangles rising up on one side. Wrap it around the birthday person's head to size it, then tape the two ends together.

2. Write "Birthday King" or "Birthday Queen" on the crown.

3. Let the birthday person wear the crown all day.

Helpful Hint: As an additional honor, seat the birthday person at the head of the table when you eat. Give him a special "Birthday King" or "Birthday Queen" plate to eat from.

Birthday Song

Why not enhance the King or Queen for a Day theme (page 110) with a special birthday song? Writing the words to your song might be a collaborative family effort, but you could also commission the most creative and talented family member to write the words.

Materials:
• Paper and pen or pencil

Directions:
1. Decide whether this will be a collaborative effort or if you'll have one creative family member write the song.

2. Choose a tune:
   • You could write special words to "Happy Birthday."
   • You could write special birthday words to a favorite family tune.
   • If you have a family member who not only writes but also composes music, you could have her write an original tune for your birthday song.

3. Write the words. Remember, they should not refer to one particular member of the family. You're going to be singing this song every time a family member has a birthday.

4. Decide when your birthday song will be sung. You could sing it to the birthday person when he comes to breakfast. You could sing it instead of or in addition to "Happy Birthday" when you carry the cake into the dining room. Or you could sing the song while placing the Birthday Hat (page 111) on the birthday person's head, or at any other suitable time.

Helpful Hint: Make sure all family members like the tune and words. Vote if necessary.

Family Anniversary

A wedding marks the beginning of a new family. Why should your wedding anniversary be an occasion celebrated by the parents only? You could invite the whole family to celebrate with you—as you did the day you were married.

Materials: Vary according to how you decide to celebrate

Directions:

1. Prior to the actual anniversary, decide how your family wants to celebrate the occasion. In part this will depend on when the anniversary takes place: a workday, school day, weekend, or holiday. It might be evening-only or an all-day celebration.

2. Start with a festive breakfast to launch the day.

3. Organize a special dinner. Options include a fancy restaurant, backyard picnic, barbecue, or sumptuous dining room feast with the good china.

4. Perhaps you'll want to look over old photo albums or watch family videos, or reminisce about the times you've shared since the founding of the family.

5. This is also a good time for telling family stories, especially the one about how the parents met.

6. Any special treat your family enjoys is appropriate, too, as long as it encompasses the whole family.

Helpful Hint: If the parents want to celebrate more intimately after the party—sharing a bottle of champagne for two and continuing from there—there's no reason why they shouldn't!

Celebrating Half-Holidays

Your family's special customs and traditions set you apart from other families. Add to this the fact that every family loves to celebrate, and you have two good reasons to enjoy half-holidays.

Materials:
- A calendar
- Vary according to the holiday

Directions:
1. Go through a calendar and mark the dates that fall six months before major holidays, for example: June 25 (Half-Christmas), July 1 (Half-New Year's), the fourth Thursday in May (Half-Thanksgiving), and August 14 (Half-Valentine's Day).
2. Also mark the half-birthdays of all family members.
3. Celebrate each holiday in a way that is appropriate, although you may want to be more restrained than you would on the full holiday:
   - For Half-New Year's, you might review your resolutions and see how well you've been keeping them, and perhaps make new ones or reaffirm your resolve to keep the original ones.
   - For Half-Christmas, you won't send cards to nonfamily members and you probably won't put up a tree, but you can exchange presents. You can also enjoy a traditional Christmas dinner with special family fixings and even some homemade eggnog.
   - For Half-Valentine's Day, make homemade valentine cards for each other.
   - For half-birthdays, have each family member give the birthday person a gift.
   - For Half-Thanksgiving, enjoy a traditional Thanksgiving dinner.
4. Half-Independence Day falls three days after New Year's, but there's no reason you shouldn't celebrate it if you want to. Similarly, you could celebrate the half-holiday of any other festive or solemn occasion you want (Half-Memorial Day, Half-Halloween, even Half-President's Day).

Helpful Hint: Even though your kids may try to convince you otherwise, these celebrations should not be used as an excuse to skip school.

Holidays

Passover: Seder

Passover seder is a wonderful celebration that includes the whole family. One family I know added an interesting twist to the hiding of the afikomen: They played "hot and cold" with their daughter as she searched for the hidden matzo!

Easter: Dye and Decorate Eggs

Why not write the family name on some of your eggs? Or dye them in your family's favorite colors? Really artistic people can even try to reproduce the family crest!

Easter: Make and Decorate Hats

Nobody said Easter finery has to be "for real." What's wrong with outlandish paper hats? Make some wacky Easter bonnets and have an afternoon fashion show on Easter Sunday!

Mother's/Father's/Grandparents' Day: Tribute

In advance of the special day, have each family member tape-record a tribute to the honored person. Take turns—using the same tape. Include heartfelt speeches of appreciation, poems, songs, and so on.

Mother's/Father's/Grandparents' Day: Homemade Cards

Homemade cards are much more meaningful than store-bought ones. They say exactly what you feel. And everyone will know the sentiment comes straight from the heart.

Mother's/Father's/Grandparents' Day: Write a Poem

Don't stop at writing a card for the special day—write a poem. Never mind if the meter's off a little or the rhyme's imperfect. It really is the thought that counts—and the knowledge that *you* wrote it.

Grandparents' Day: Making Contact

Phone calls are easier than writing something out for grandparents, but after the kids hang up, all Grandma and Grandpa have left is their memory of the conversation. This is good, but you should also have the kids send a package—a letter, a paper from school, a picture, crafts made in school—anything meaningful that the kids created themselves and grandparents can cherish forever.

May Day/Earth Day/Arbor Day: Plant a Tree

Celebrate any of these holidays by planting a tree. Plant it in your backyard and watch it grow as your family grows. Or plant it in a public place and have the secret joy of knowing, every time you see it, that it's your family's tree. Get permission if necessary, of course.

May Day/Earth Day/Arbor Day: Neighborhood Cleanup

Your family members are citizens of more than just your own household. You're citizens of the world. Help clean up that little corner of the world—your neighborhood. Whether you do it on your own or organize other families to help you, picking up trash on your block is a good way to celebrate any of these holidays.

Memorial Day: Remembering Loved Ones

Hold a memorial service for family, friends, even pets who are no longer on this earth. The service can take place in your backyard, weather permitting. If you live in an apartment, try the local park.

Memorial Day: Memory Album

If you have family members, friends, or pets who have died, how about compiling a memory album for that person or animal? Combine a few photos selected from your main photo albums with handwritten or typed remembrances. Compile the album the first year. Each year after that, revisit the album and let it spark memories that you can share with loved ones.

Independence Day: Family or Neighborhood Parade

Not every parade has to be as big as Macy's Thanksgiving parade. Simply organize the families on your block, decorate your cars, and drive around your neighborhood streets in your very own Independence Day celebration!

Independence Day: Plant a Red, White, and Blue Garden

Plant the flowers early so that they'll bloom in American flag colors by the time Independence Day arrives. If you're really dedicated to this project, plant the flowers in a pattern that resembles the stars and stripes of our flag.

Halloween: Make Costumes

In generations past, nobody bought Halloween costumes. They were all homemade. And you know what? It was fun. Assembling and creating the costumes was nearly as much fun as trick-or-treating. Honor these traditions by making your own costume this year.

Halloween: Decorate

Get into the Halloween spirit by cutting out black spiders and orange jack-o'-lanterns from construction paper. Hang handkerchiefs that look like ghosts and decorate your windows at least a week or so before the holiday.

Halloween: Tell Spooky Stories

When the kids are done trick-or-treating, cap off the evening with a round of ghost stories in front of the fireplace. Then put out the fire, leave one lamp burning low, and let the kids camp out for the night on the living room floor in their sleeping bags. They'll help each other ward off evil spirits from stories that have spooked them.

Halloween: Carve Pumpkins

How about carving the back of your jack-o'-lantern with the family name or initial? As the front of the pumpkin casts a glowing, toothy grin out the window at passersby, the back will glow into the house with your family's name.

Thanksgiving: Caroling

Traditionally, the day after Thanksgiving initiates the holiday season. Why not borrow a Christmas tradition and take your family Thanksgiving caroling this year? As you walk up and down your block stopping at neighbors' doors, you can sing traditional hymns like "Come, Ye Thankful People, Come," or "We Gather Together." Don't forget songs like "Over the River and through the Woods," too.

Thanksgiving: Giving Thanks

Does your family know the true meaning of Thanksgiving? Or is it just that holiday where you get off from school and watch football and eat turkey? Spend time remembering the people you're thankful for, and give everyone a chance to communicate gratitude to the entire family.

Thanks*Giving*

Does your family have extended family nearby who gather with you for Thanksgiving dinner? If not, consider making the holiday truly meaningful by volunteering your time and energy at a free Thanksgiving dinner for the less fortunate. These meals may be served by an organization such as the Salvation Army, by a church or temple, or by a local restaurant. Find out which organizations in your community need help.

Thanksgiving: Holiday Tablecloth

Make a special holiday tablecloth. Using permanent fine-line markers, draw designs on a white or light-colored sheet. All family members should write or draw on the cloth. They should draw an appropriate picture or write sentiments such as "I am thankful for my family and friends."

Hanukkah: Make a Menorah and Candles

Though a functional menorah may be beyond your family's ability to make, you can make a decorative one out of construction paper. Cut the paper to match the menorah design, using yellow paper for flames. Tape it in your window and display it proudly.

Hanukkah: Tell the Story

Your kids light the candles, play with the dreidel, and enjoy the presents—but do they know the true meaning of Hanukkah? Do they know the story of the Maccabees? Do they know that the letters on the dreidel stand for "A great miracle happened there"? Tell them the history of the holiday to make the celebration more meaningful.

Kwanzaa: Make Your Own Gifts

Kwanzaa is a relatively new holiday that celebrates the traditional family values of unity, self-determination, collective work and responsibility, cooperative economics, purpose, creativity, and faith. Encourage family members to make their own personal gifts to give each other, instead of relying on store-bought gifts.

Christmas: Make Ornaments

Sometime before you buy your Christmas tree, devote an evening to ornament making. Each member of the family should contribute one ornament per year. You could do any of the following, depending on your kids' ages: Take a plain glass ball ornament and decorate it with sequins or fake jewels. Paint decorations on it or write personal sentiments with a thin-line permanent marker. You could also take a real pine cone, attach a hook to it, and spray it with silver paint or artificial snow. A five-year-old could draw a face on a snowman (with crayon) that Mom or Dad has cut out of cardboard.

Christmas: Early Santa

One set of parents I know—eager to sleep later than 3:30 on Christmas morning—allowed their kids to open their presents on Christmas Eve. With the cooperation of a nearby uncle, they coordinated dinner out with an early visit from Santa. While parents and kids had a special Christmas Eve dinner at a restaurant, the dad's brother let himself in and spread out the presents under the tree. "Oh look—Santa's been here!" the surprised parents exclaimed when they returned with the kids.

Of course, the kids were baffled, even skeptical, but the parents explained that Santa has many houses to visit, and all on Christmas, so naturally he has to take care of some houses early. They ate dinner out every Christmas Eve after that, so that Santa would always visit them early!

Christmas: Family Thank-You Book

Keep a record of gifts received by every family member, or at least those received from people outside the immediate family. Record them as you get them, listing both the gift and the giver. Make a big check mark next to the listing as you send off a thank-you note for the gift. This way there'll never be any question about who gave Lisa the yellow sweater, what Aunt Ginny gave Dan for Christmas, or whether Robbie wrote to Grandma to thank her for the gift.

Christmas: Make Presents

A homemade gift can be more meaningful than a store-bought one, especially when the gift is for Grandma or Grandpa or another close relative. Homemade is also the way to go for a child on a tight budget. A few weeks before Christmas, have the whole family devote one evening to making gifts together. Put Christmas music on the stereo, turn the tree lights on, and have fun!

Christmas: Make Gift Wrap

Homemade gift wrap adds a nice touch to your holiday gifts. There are several ways to make gift wrap. You can decorate aluminum foil or brown wrapping paper with fine-line permanent markers and stick-on stars. You could also cut up last year's Christmas cards and glue appropriate pictures onto brown wrapping paper.

Christmas: Bake and Decorate Cookies

The whole family can bake cookies that will taste delicious and make great gifts. It's just another activity to enhance the Christmas spirit filling your hearts and homes.

Christmas: Write Your Own Carol

Elsewhere in this book, I've discussed writing your own words to an existing song, or writing a song from scratch if you have a composer in the family. You can do that for Christmas, too. Why not write your own Christmas carol? Think how special it will make you feel to know you're singing a song that's unique to your family—especially if your family goes out caroling!

Christmas: Old Toy Exchange

Shortly before Christmas, you'll probably encourage the kids to give away toys they no longer play with, to make room for the new ones they're about to get. But some kids resist giving anything away. If you're tired of seeing toys that never get played with, you might be able to get the kids to trade with their friends. This won't solve the space problem, but if you have a toy exchange at the start of the school Christmas break, it will give the kids "new" toys to play with during the break before they get their Christmas haul. You could also encourage the kids to donate their unwanted toys to charity.

New Year's: Resolutions with a Twist

Rather than making New Year's resolutions, do something different. Let every family member write, on separate pieces of paper, the habits or behaviors you know you should improve. Then, with great solemnity, gather in front of the fireplace. One by one, have each member read aloud what they've written. When finished, have them toss the sheet into the fire. Up in flames goes the sheet of paper—and the bad habit with it.

New Year's Eve at Home

Maybe you hate driving on New Year's Eve, and getting a sitter is just too much of a hassle. Maybe the prices at local restaurants are enough to set you back a week's pay, and you're not up for another New Year's Eve party out. Why not stay home with the kids and make it a family occasion?

Let the kids stay up as late as they want. Let them toot noisemakers and bang the bottoms of pots. Take time to look back at the past year—and ahead at the year to come. You can reminisce merrily or take time for quiet reflection.

New Year's: Family Predictions

Here's a fun idea: Each New Year's Day, have every family member write down what he or she thinks is going to happen to the family— or the individual family members—in the year ahead. Store the predictions somewhere. Next New Year's Day, have everyone read the predictions they made last New Year's. Have any of them come true? Have any of them missed the mark so widely that they're funny?

New Year's: Plan for the Year Ahead

New Year's is a good time to look ahead and think of family plans. Do you have thoughts about your family vacation this year? Do the kids want to go to a different summer camp or vacation spot? Is this the year you move, redecorate, repaint, get a new car, or buy a boat? Do the kids have a particular wish or plan in mind? Ideas may not be feasible ("No, we can't get a dog—we already have two cats"), but at least let all family members express themselves.

Index

The Preschooler's Busy Book

by Trish Kuffner
Illustrated by Laurel Aiello

The book contains 365 activities (one for each day of the year) for three- to six-year-olds using things found around the home. It shows parents and daycare providers how to:

• prevent boredom during even the longest stretches of bad weather, with ideas for indoor play, kitchen activities, and arts and crafts projects;

• save money by making homemade paint, playdough, craft clay, glue, paste, and other arts and crafts supplies;

• stimulate a child's natural curiosity with fun reading, math, and science activities.

Order #6055 $9.95

The Kids' Pick-A-Party Book

by Penny Warner
Illustrated by Laurel Aiello

Here are 50 creative theme parties to make
birthdays and other celebrations so much fun,
kids won't want to leave. Warner provides
ideas for invitations, decorations, costumes,
games, activities, food, and party favors to
help parents make celebrations memorable
and entertaining.

Order #6090 $9.00

Pick A Party

by Patty Sachs

Here's the "bible" for party planners. Party expert Patty Sachs has included 145 party themes—more than any other book—to help you turn holidays, birthdays, showers, and evenings with friends or family into special occasions.

Order #6085 $9.00

The Best Party Book

by Penny Warner

Penny Warner provides creative ideas for invitations, decorations, refreshments, games, prizes, and party favors to turn your parties into memorable celebrations. Includes ideas for seasonal parties (Halloween, Christmas, New Year's, and more), family events (birthdays, anniversaries, reunions, and more), even special TV events (the Academy Awards and the Super Bowl).

Order #6089 $9.00

Look for Meadowbrook Press books at your local bookseller. You may also order books by using the form printed below.

Order Form

Qty.	Title	Author	Order #	Unit Cost (U.S. $)	Total
	Baby Play & Learn	Warner, P.	1275	$9.00	
	Best Party Book	Warner, P.	6089	$9.00	
	Dinner Party Cookbook	Brown, K.	6035	$9.00	
	For Better and For Worse	Lansky, B.	4000	$7.00	
	Games People Play	Warner, P.	6093	$8.00	
	Happy Anniversary!	Kring, R.	6041	$9.00	
	Joy of Grandparenting	Sherins/Holleman	3502	$7.00	
	Joy of Marriage	Dodds, M. & B.	3504	$7.00	
	Joy of Parenthood	Blaustone, J	3500	$7.00	
	Kids' Holiday Fun	Warner, P.	6000	$12.00	
	Kids' Outdoor Parties	Warner, P.	6045	$8.00	
	Kids' Party Cookbook	Warner, P.	2435	$12.00	
	Kids' Party Games and Activities	Warner, P.	6095	$12.00	
	Kids' Pick-a-Party Book	Warner, P.	6090	$9.00	
	Lovesick	Lansky, B.	4045	$7.00	
	Mommy's Little Helper Christmas Crafts	MacGregor, C.	2445	$8.00	
	Mommy's Little Helper Cookbook	Brown, K.	2455	$9.00	
	Pick A Party	Sachs, P.	6085	$9.00	
	Pick-A-Party Cookbook	Sachs, P.	6086	$11.00	
	Preschooler's Busy Book	Kuffner, T.	6055	$9.95	
	Toddler's Busy Book	Kuffner, T.	1250	$9.95	
	When You Were a Baby	Haley, A.	1391	$8.00	
				Subtotal	
			Shipping and Handling (see below)		
			MN residents add 6.5% sales tax		
				Total	

YES! Please send me the books indicated above. Add $2.00 shipping and handling for the first book and 50¢ for each additional book. Add $2.50 to total for books shipped to Canada. Overseas postage will be billed. Allow up to four weeks for delivery. Send check or money order payable to Meadowbrook Press. No cash or CODs, please. Prices subject to change without notice. **Quantity discounts available upon request.**

Send book(s) to:

Name _____ Address_____

City _____ State ___ Zip _____ Telephone (____)_____

Payment via:

❏ Check or money order payable to Meadowbrook Press

❏ Visa (for orders over $10.00 only) ❏ MasterCard (for orders over $10.00 only)

Account # _____ Signature _____ Exp. Date _____

You can also phone or fax us with a credit card order.

A *FREE* Meadowbrook Press catalog is available upon request.

Mail to: Meadowbrook Press, 5451 Smetana Drive, Minnetonka, MN 55343

Phone 612-930-1100   Toll-Free 800-338-2232   Fax 612-930-1940

For more information (and fun) visit our website:
www.meadowbrookpress.com